LOVE
OF
ENEMIES

OVERTURES TO BIBLICAL THEOLOGY

A series of studies in biblical theology designed to explore fresh dimensions of research and to suggest ways in which the biblical heritage may address contemporary culture

Editors

WALTER BRUEGGEMANN, Professor of Old Testament at Eden Theological Seminary, St. Louis, Missouri

JOHN R. DONAHUE, S.J., Professor of New Testament at the Jesuit School of Theology, Berkeley, California

The
Way
to
Peace

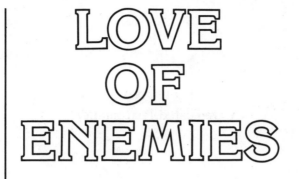

LOVE
OF
ENEMIES

WILLIAM KLASSEN

FORTRESS PRESS   Philadelphia

TO DONA
A Dedicated Peacemaker

Biblical quotations, unless otherwise noted, are from the Revised Standard Version of the Bible, copyright 1946, 1952, © 1971, 1973 by the Division of Christian Education of the National Council of the Churches of Christ in the U.S.A. and are used by permission.

Library of Congress Cataloging in Publication Data

Klassen, William.
  Love of enemies.

  (Overtures to Biblical theology; 15)
  Bibliography: p.
  Includes index.
  1. Peace—Biblical teaching. 2. Love (Theology)—
Biblical teaching. I. Title. II. Series.
  BS680.P4K57 1984   261.8'73   84-47927
  ISBN 0-8006-1539-5 (pbk.)

K968D84   Printed in the United States of America 1-1539

Contents

Editor's Foreword

This examination of the relation of love of enemies to questions of war and peace in the Jewish and Christian tradition comes at a time when overtures to those who care seriously for the biblical tradition can be spurned only with great risk. In recent years issues of war and peace have reached an unprecedented level of public discussion, epitomized by the Pastoral Letter, *The Challenge of Peace: God's Promise and Our Response* issued by the Roman Catholic Bishops of the United States on May 3, 1983, and by the *Statement on Peace and Justice* of the Sixth Assembly of the World Council of Churches meeting in Vancouver, British Columbia from July 24–August 10, 1983 (*Gathering for Life*, Official Report of the Sixth Assembly of the World Council of Churches, pp. 130–38). In the above statements the biblical heritage is used to question the morality of the arms race and of nuclear escalation. Conversely, the Bible is invoked by national leaders to justify a militant posture against adversaries. The need for solid biblical study is clear, and, as William Klassen notes, there has been a great neglect of the themes "peace" and "love of enemies" by professional biblical scholars, especially in the English-speaking world.

Love of Enemies: The Way to Peace will not address every text in the Bible which treats of these themes, nor will it address every question readers bring to these texts. Such a task is too vast for any one volume. What it does is to locate significant statements in their historical and literary context and thus provides a solid exegetical basis for a theology of peace. By giving detailed attention to the Hellenistic background of biblical thought and to Jewish literature of the intertestamental period, Klassen's work will shed new light on some old and familiar texts and bring to light some which have been overlooked. His research also counters many of the stereotypes concerning what the Hebrew Bible says on war and love of enemies and challenges facile claims of uniqueness attributed to many statements in the New Testament. This work will hopefully precipitate continued reflection and debate in both the academic community and in the churches.

William Klassen brings to this study a distinctive background and training. Nourished in the Mennonite tradition and trained in New Testament at Princeton, he has taught at the Mennonite Seminary in Elkhart, Indiana, at the University of Manitoba, and has been a visiting professor at the University of Notre Dame and at New York Theological Seminary. For two decades he has done research and writing on issues of social concern and especially on peace. He has chaired the Seminar on Pauline Ethics of the Society of Biblical Literature (1979–82) and the Seminar on "The Context of New Testament Ethics" for the Society for New Testament Studies. This latter position brought him into contact with the leading European thinkers on issues of peace such as Luise Schottroff, and his research in Israel (1973–74) enabled him to become engaged with the challenge of the biblical statements on peace in a land at war. Recently he has been appointed Dean of the Inter-Faith Academy of Peace of the Ecumenical Institute in Jerusalem. Scholarship and a wealth of personal engagement have both left their imprint on this book.

This work should challenge religious people today to a *metanoia* or change of heart no less serious than racism confronted them in the sixties or sexism in the seventies. Too often concern for issues of war and peace surfaces with renewed consciousness of the imminence of nuclear destruction, only to be muted for another decade. The historical peace churches are often viewed as marginal by mainline denominations, and those who write and speak on peace are often a solitary witness. The past two decades have seen a significant retrieval of the biblical heritage in a number of areas. Encounter with the God of the Exodus who led a people from oppression and sent the prophets to defend the defenseless has spawned a "theology of liberation." When it turned to full human liberation, this theology mandated "depatriarchalizing" the biblical tradition. The time has now come for the Christian churches to "demilitarize" this same tradition. Klassen's research over the years and his active engagement in issues of peace and war, the fruit of which we now share, are an invitation and a challenge to join this enterprise.

JOHN R. DONAHUE, S.J.

Preface

Since 1961 I have tried to read every article, monograph, and book on the topic of peace and love your enemies. From the first time I read a scholarly paper on this topic in 1961 till the present, I have been grateful for the encouragement of numerous people: Krister Stendahl, Abraham J. Malherbe, and Howard Charles. Each has raised critical questions while continuing to affirm the validity of the question being addressed. I am also deeply grateful for colleagues in the Seminar on "The Context of New Testament Ethics" of the Society for New Testament Studies which for five years looked at various issues, including the issues of peace and the command to love your enemies. This seminar, which met from 1977–82, brought together scholars from behind the iron curtain and from the Orient, as well as from the whole spectrum of New Testament scholarship. I am particularly grateful to Professors Ernst Käsemann and Luise Schottroff for their animated participation and for the leadership the latter provided as we became involved in the issues of peace and war.

The Ecumenical Institute at Tantur, Israel, graciously provided me with an excellent context in which to write and think about these issues. The Ecole Biblique generously allowed me the use of their excellent library in Jerusalem. Both the University of Manitoba, and the Social Sciences and Humanities Research Council of Canada supported me during the time of research. Simon Fraser University has provided me with a context in which to complete this work, and I joyfully acknowledge my debt especially to Jack Blaney who sees development in its larger wholeness. His warm support is deeply valued.

When invited to submit a manuscript for the Overtures series I was honored but also keenly aware that much of what I had discovered in ancient sources would need to be omitted in order to meet the specifications of this series.

In preparing this book it has been a pleasure to work with John Donahue, S.J. and the editors of Fortress Press. Surely we have made some considerable progress in ecumenical work when a work on peace by a Mennonite author is edited by a Jesuit and published by a Lutheran publishing house!

Additional assistance in the editorial process was provided by my wife, Dona, who often laid aside her own editorial duties to listen to my ideas and went through the whole manuscript carefully. It is due to her careful editing that it reads as well as it does. She also has demonstrated her commitment to the Pauline affirmation that the call to peace is nowhere more deeply felt than in the home (1 Cor. 7:15). She values peace and knows how to share it. My parents, too, taught me much about peace as they reared their brood of fifteen. Who knows how many of the convictions which I acquired through a study of ancient texts are supported by early childhood contacts: mother's quiet strength and father's simple adherence to the literal text of the Holy Book?

Unless otherwise noted, the translations of and references to the Babylonian Talmud are from *The Babylonian Talmud,* ed. I. Epstein, 35 volumes (London: Soncino Press, 1932–52). Classical texts and other ancient works are cited from the Loeb Classical Library (Cambridge: Harvard Univ. Press; London: William Heinemann), unless otherwise noted. Certain other texts have been translated by me or the source of translation has been acknowledged.

Abbreviations

ATR	*Anglican Theological Review*
B.C.E.	Before the Common Era (= B.C.)
b.	*Babylonian Talmud*
BWANT	Beiträge zur Wissenschaft vom Alten und Neuen Testament
CBC	Canadian Broadcasting Corporation
CBQ	*Catholic Biblical Quarterly*
C.E.	Common Era (= A.D.)
ET	English Translator
ExpTim	*Expository Times*
HTR	*Harvard Theological Review*
JB	Jerusalem Bible
JBL	*Journal of Biblical Literature*
JE	*Jewish Encyclopedia*
KHCAT	Keil Handkommentar zum Alten Testament
LCL	Loeb Classical Library
m.	*Midrash*
NEB	New English Bible
NIV	New International Version
NovT	*Novum Testamentum*
NTS	*New Testament Studies*
QS	Qumran Serekh = *Manual of Discipline*
SBLSCS	Society of Biblical Literature Septuagint and Cognate Studies
SEÅ	*Svensk exegetisk årsbok*
SVF	H. von Arnim, *Stoicorum Veterum Fragmenta* (1903–)

TDNT	*Theological Dictionary of the New Testament*
TDOT	*Theological Dictionary of the Old Testament*
TLZ	*Theologische Literaturzeitung*
ZNW	*Zeitschrift für die neutestamentliche Wissenschaft*
ZTK	*Zeitschrift für Theologie und Kirche*

"It is the duty of those who study the scriptures
not only to become expert themselves, but also
to use their scholarship for the benefit of the
outside world through both the spoken and the
written word."

(Preface to the Book of *Sirach*)

Introduction:
A Word of Peace
in a World at War

LISTENING TO THE WORD

Three distinct concerns influence my reflections on peace. There is *first* of all my responsibility as a biblical scholar to the Word. It is incumbent upon me to listen to what it has to say. When I investigated what scholars have written about the biblical concept of peace, I found very little. No monograph or scholarly book in English on peace in the New Testament exists, to my knowledge. A concordance reveals, however, that the reason for this lack of scholarly interest in peace in the New Testament has nothing to do with lack of evidence. The fact that popular writings on the topic abound and that such scholarly books on peace exist in other languages can only lead to the conclusion that Anglo-Saxon scholars, myself included, have not listened to the Word in the way it deserves.

Too often we think that we have listened to the Word when we have merely spoken appreciatively of it or quoted it. In public life this is a constant temptation.

A few weeks after President Reagan had proclaimed 1983 The Year of the Bible he told a meeting of the National Association of Evangelicals in Orlando, Florida that belief in God should make Americans join him in opposing a nuclear freeze and pressing for a vast build-up in U.S. weapons. "There is sin and evil in the world and we are enjoined by Scripture and the Lord Jesus to oppose it with all our might." He described Soviet communism as the "focus of evil in the modern world" and those who favor a mutual freeze on new nuclear weapons ignore "the aggressive instincts of an evil empire."[1]

We have in the past year been warned (in Canada by our Prime

1

Minister) that it is dangerous for theologians and biblical scholars to meddle in the complicated matters of economics and international conflict. After all we are not specialists. No such reserve seems to characterize politicians when they want to appeal to the Bible or to the resources of religion. Indeed people in the churches are often flattered when politicians appeal to the Bible even when such appeals are less than a compliment to the normal use of our intelligence. Harry Truman wrote to his wife Bess about his cold war obligations: "We've got to organize the people who believe in honor and the Golden Rule to win the world back to peace and Christianity."[2] The Canadian Prime Minister during World War II considered it "fortunate the use of the [atomic] bomb should have been upon the Japanese rather than upon the white races of Europe." Later he signed the order in council to deport Japanese Canadians to Japan after the war defending it with the unctuous words: "May I say that we have . . . followed that ancient precept of doing justice but also loving mercy."[3] Fortunately he did not add the further blasphemy, "and walk humbly with our God."

It is refreshing to have public figures declare openly what the religious basis for their actions are. Then a dialogue can begin. Likewise the church can only benefit from placing its value system into the public arena so that the changes it calls for and the loyalties it follows can be debated publicly. One can go even further: it is essential for any fruitful Bible study, for any quest for the will of God, that a study of the past—including what we believe happened in our past—be conducted alongside of the fullest scrutiny of what is happening in our world today.

When the study of the Bible became my profession, and I had the opportunity of looking at other theological traditions, it became increasingly clear that the center of the search for peace is "the meaning of Jesus Christ and his teaching." Throughout the years this question of how the Bible can speak with authority became and remains the center of my quest. For it became evident, that whatever one might find in the Bible, if the literary approach in interpretation is inadequate and Christ as center is missing then our hearing of the text is inadequate.

At the outset I register my commitment to the consensual approach. Consensus is our goal. If, however, we do not attain that goal it does not mean that we become paralyzed. We can have in the church, for example, a group that has held out for a very strong confrontational approach to the question of disarmament, but has not been able to get its denomination or even its subgroup behind it. Although consensus is lacking, it is not necessary for that group to hold back its convictions. It can test them in the field. This is clearly what Martin Luther King, Jr., did for the Christian church in the twentieth century. It has also been done by Cesar Chavez, Thomas Merton, Daniel Berrigan, and the South American bishops. Broadly speaking, this book approaches the Bible from the viewpoint of biblical realism which seeks to take the categories of the Bible with utmost seriousness.

The critical question, therefore, is what is the message of the Bible on peace for us? The church is asking that question on many fronts. It is a question which has become far more urgent for us since the first atomic bomb was dropped. We remember that vividly and have watched with horror as, in the intervening years, we have not turned our backs on this monstrous deed but, instead, have pursued ever more devastating ways to destroy ourselves, as if our salvation lay in such destruction! The church, too, has been slow and inconsistent in its coping with this new fact.

The question uppermost then in our minds as we search, is what bearing does this new human capacity to destroy ourselves have on our understanding of the peace which Christ has brought? We cannot take lightly the fact that a "Christian" nation was the first to invent and to use this horrendous weapon. Neither can we take lightly the fact that a "Christian" nation is the most heavily armed today; nor can we ignore the fact that a "Christian" nation shares responsibility for much of the conflict in the world today. As American journalist Anthony Lewis recently wrote about the arms race: "The terrible irony of that race is that the United States has led the way on virtually every major new development over the last thirty years, only to find itself met by the Soviet Union."[4]

It is profoundly unsettling that this conflict is fed by the claim to be following the Bible with such statements as "there are things that are more important than peace, namely, justice." Does not a large segment of Christianity see a coming war as a fulfillment of biblical prophecy? We cannot ignore the fact that in North American Christianity, Hal Lindsey and Jerry Falwell have had far more influence than have Thomas Merton and Daniel Berrigan and perhaps even Martin Luther King, Jr. The "holy war" is still very much alive among the three religions of the West: Judaism, Christianity, and Islam. Have we listened to the Word if it calls us to war?

Here we survey the importance of this theme in those religious sources that have a particular authority for the Christian community, namely, what Christians call the Old and the New Testament. With respect to the canon within the canon, I take without any apologies the New Testament as more authoritative than the Old Testament. Even within the New Testament I assume that the basis of our authority is Christology or the view that we have of Jesus. The incarnation is the key to our interpretation of the will of God for us. The way in which we understand that is illuminated by the gift of the Holy Spirit who assists us in finding the will of God. Nothing is more urgent than for the Christian community to engage seriously in that quest for the will of God, and with all the skills at its disposal to practise listening to the Word. It is a road that leads to peace.

There is no implication here of the superiority of Christianity over any other religion, certainly not of the superiority of Christianity over Judaism. The question of who is superior is a totally human question, usually an infantile one. Jesus urged his disciples to move beyond it (Mark 9:33–37; 10:35–45). In the kingdom the child has a high rank, and the servant has the highest status of all. For the Jew, obviously his religion is superior. He has chosen to live by it. To the Christian, obviously his religion is preferable, or else he would be something else. The question of superiority is about as useful as comparing spouses.

There do, however, emerge some sharp differences. This book does not address the Wars of Yahweh motif so prevalent in the Old Testament (e.g., Deut. 33:2–5, 26–29; Judges 5; Josh. 10:12–13). On the one hand, it is ignored here because it has received thorough discussion on the part of competent scholars.[5] More important, however, it does not receive thorough discussion here because it is missing in the New Testament totally. This omission is not considered accidental. The focus of the New Testament is on a better way. It is that way which we search for in this study. Judaism as such has rejected the Holy War motif, and a key figure was the prophet, Jesus of Nazareth.

Both first-century Jews and Christians shared with their pagan counterparts a commitment to benevolence rather than violence as the best expression of the human.

RESPONSIBILITY TO THE WORLD

The *second* concern which influences my reflections on peace is my responsibility to the world. During the writing of this book, many people who profess to no religion frankly expressed their puzzlement that I would, from the standpoint of religion, seek to address this issue. "Is not religion more than any one other factor responsible for the wars we have had?" one man asked me.

Karl Barth, one of the most influential theologians of our time, recognized the need to read the Bible alongside the daily newspaper. This practice drew him into a prison ministry in which he preached regularly to the "enemies" of society. Many biblical scholars today agree with Adolf Schlatter's slogan: "into the Word and into the world." They recognize that just as God's presence became manifest through the incarnation of Jesus, so, too, must the scholar always move back and forth from Word to world if the true authority and richness of the Word is to ease human pain.

As soon as we move from the Word to the world we recognize that there is an enormous difference. The Word says that Yahweh is King, and victory in battle can only be won when Yahweh fights and lays the ground rules. In the world, God does not figure at all in the conflicts that rage, except perhaps occasionally being called upon to be on one side or the other. The Word says "love your enemies," the world says "don't trust them, shoot them, bomb them," and be prepared for massive retaliation on such a scale that life on half of the earth is wiped out. Even the traditional category of a defensive war yields in the world to such terms as "pre-emptive strikes," for in modern war where matters move very quickly, such a strike may be the best defensive measure. So it is argued.

The contrast between Word and world is stark and cannot be missed today. But it takes a careful listening to the Word to find the implications of this yawning gap between what God had intended for the human race and where we are now heading. The most serious mistake we can make is to assume that in some way such matters as a thermonuclear war can be survived or, even worse, that it can in some way be seen as God's will. No act of God will bring it. If we in our folly wish to pursue a course which leads to it, God will not in the last minute intervene. God did not stop the first parents of the human race from disobeying his will, and it is not God's custom to do so now. Our minds, our hearts, and our hands activated by our wills can avoid a global disaster.

A PERSONAL PERSPECTIVE

In the *third* place, some important experiences have obviously influenced my reflections. When the atomic bomb was dropped on civilians in Japan, my major concerns were getting through high school and growing wheat on the family farm. During the war years an "enemy" Japanese family was deported from British Columbia to live and work on our farm. As we worked together we formed strong ties. Later, the question was often debated whether wheat should be sold to the enemy—that enemy being variously defined as Russia, China, Cuba, and, during the twenty years I lived in the United States, even such neutral countries as India who were enemies precisely because they claimed neutrality!

The concept of loving one's enemy first occurred to me during those years. It seemed incomprehensible to me that anyone who had read Jesus and Paul on this topic could insist that Canada should not sell wheat to countries who needed it. During the decade from 1958–68 I was increasingly caught up in the discrepancy that existed between the public affirmation that a given country was Christian (a strange notion!) and the type of government policy which would deny food to hungry people. The conviction sharpened in my mind that we have a prior obligation: the obligation to be human to our fellow humans.

That conviction is grounded in my religious commitment, specifically in the belief that Jesus of Nazareth was truly human and that it is possible to embody his humanity today. For the Christian church Jesus is not only human but also the unique authoritative Word of God to humanity. He is affirmed as the Christ of God. In Jesus all the treasures of wisdom are found. The more he has been studied, the more the conclusion has emerged that what he taught about loving enemies is fundamental, not peripheral, to the church and its understanding of its own existence. Indeed it is fundamental to the survival of the human race. Unless humans learn to live with their enemies, indeed, unless we learn to love our enemies, our days on this earth are numbered.

The ethics of Jesus cannot be imposed upon anyone. His way must be freely chosen. Those who accept Jesus as Lord have a peculiar perspective from which to approach this evidence. We make certain affirmations which are central to the good news. Without that there is no Christian church. It begins with the good news that while we were still enemies of God and estranged from him, in Jesus God showed us that he loves us nonetheless. So Jesus is God's way of loving his enemies, shown perhaps most vividly in the fact that Jesus spent most of his time with God's "enemies," not his "friends."

Furthermore, Jesus taught that those who follow him should likewise love their enemies (Matt. 5:44; Luke 6:28–35). The unanimous opinion of scholars that this word does in fact go back to Jesus himself, the evidence that the early church took it with utmost seriousness, the strikingly unique way in which this teaching cuts against the grain of popular morality in his day as in ours, are all taken up here. What emerges is the conviction that the church cannot ignore Jesus' teaching of the love of enemies if it wishes to be true to itself.

Jesus nowhere prescribes regular church attendance or the tithe. He did not issue detailed instructions on sexual morality for his followers or whether they should drink wine, or dance. He *does* tell them that they are to love their enemies. The more this fact comes home to us, the more any form of Christianity which does not take this teaching seriously is called into question.

Judged in this light, the most popular forms of Christianity today stand condemned. Take, for instance, that form of Christianity represented by the Moral Majority. Since loving the enemy is conspicuously absent in its "gospel" it has to be termed false and those who proclaim it designated as false prophets. The ease with which they identify America with Christianity and the fact that they do not follow Jesus in teaching release from hate, supports that judgment. In the Bible the true prophets soon found themselves expelled from the presence of the king, for they refused to ally themselves with the king or tell him what he wanted to hear.

Every popular form of Christianity must be tested by this standard:

What are the elements of the Christian faith which run counter to popular morality? How is the truly human aspect of Christianity being expressed? There were denominations in the United States who refused to listen to the State Department when it raised objections to their efforts to help Cuba in a hurricane aftermath; there were Christians in the United States who insisted on helping the North Vietnamese even while United States foreign policy dictated that Christians in the United States could not love their enemies! In such actions authentic Christianity came to expression and the vitality of the church was reaffirmed.

During those years I was struck also by the embodiment of the motif of the love of enemies in the life of Martin Luther King, Jr. It stands as one of the strongest signals in our century that Christianity is not dead. What Jesus taught about being human to one's fellow lives on. It was hard for King to learn the meaning of that teaching, even harder no doubt for him to maintain it so steadfastly till the end. But who can deny that he learned it well and taught it to us—black and white together—both by his life and death?

A major impetus in King's learning that teaching and applying it so skillfully was Mahatma Gandhi, whose own dedication to non-violence was so Christ-like, although Gandhi did not consider himself a Christian. What a paradox that God should call us back to this ethical imperative through the efforts of those whom white people often despised: the Asians and the blacks. The oppressed taught the oppressors what it meant to be under the rule of Christ.

I was furthermore deeply affected by the radical response to the command of Jesus from another unexpected area, such outstanding lay leaders as Dorothy Day, Gordon Zahn, and Jim Douglas, as well as from the monastic and priestly orders of the Catholic church—Thomas Merton, Daniel and Philip Berrigan—and from the deeply sensitive organizer of farm laborers, the Chicano, Cesar Chavez.[6] The presence of such diverse witnesses assures some people that Christ is still alive and is a source of hope.

The coming together of Word and world took place most dramatically during a year (1973–74) in Israel: the first (and I hope, last) time I lived in a country where one could hear the sound of war. Energetic and lively discussions were held with Professor David Flusser. There were times when we disagreed in matters of interpretation, and it was clear that issues of war and peace were even more urgent for him than they were for me. What he taught me above all was the Jewishness of Jesus. During the war when we wept together and lamented the futility of so much human bloodshed throughout history, we were drawn together in search for a better way in our common revulsion of violence. Moreover, in addition to our shared abhorrence of the immorality of violence and our joint conviction that violence generally results only in more violence, we affirmed the importance of the love command. Throughout, Professor Flusser was of invaluable assistance to me in locating new sources, reinterpreting well-known sources, and in providing evidence that in spite of much human hatred and bloodshed Christians and Jews have a common heritage of placing the love commandment central to human conduct.

One day during the war, Professor and Mrs. Flusser had been to Tantur for dinner. As I bade him farewell after an animated discussion about the war and Christian response to it he said: "Your people too were persecuted and killed in the sixteenth century, were they not?" When I said yes, his eyes filled with tears and we hugged each other as he said in the language of our discourse: "Wir müssen doch einen besseren Weg finden!" ("We must find a better way!")

This book is written in the hope that we may find this better way and walk it. In human history the approach of loving our enemies has always been rejected because of the risk involved. We are often reminded that people in our century, as well as in the first, who took this approach of love paid for it with their lives. Surely even more people have lost their lives by hating their enemies. After so many centuries of bloody wars, we may be prepared to look at alternatives.

The specific alternative suggested here is that we take seriously the combination of two topics which I see as related in Hebrew and Christian scriptures: love for the enemy and the achievement of peace. I do not see peace as purely internal, nor do I see loving one's enemies as restricted to a personal enemy. The reader may at times wonder why these two themes are brought together and why so much time is given to the topic of vengeance. The answer is that the sources, in my judgment, force us to see them thus. Naturally, I shall welcome from my scholarly colleagues, as well as from any thinking person, a reasoned critique of both my method of inquiry and also my conclusions. I do ask, however, that you give this arrangement of material a careful scrutiny. For I am convinced that in these ominous days, when biblical scholars have not been exactly at the forefront of those who seek to make this world a better and safer place to live, approaches should not be rejected simply because they do not follow traditional patterns.

It is also time to be emancipated from an approach which seeks merely to find a word and study it without looking at a wider context in which it appears and the agenda which lies behind it. It has been necessary to pay attention to such important human categories as "vengeance" for they are still alive and strong among us. I am also convinced that one of the reasons why we have not listened to the Word in this area is that we have lacked faith in God's rule over the world. Surely here both Jew and Christian share a common conviction: that sovereign above all that humans do, God rules. That conviction can lead us to rape the earth in our search for wealth and a high standard of living; it can cause us even to play with weapons which defy the imagination. For never having used them, we cannot even imagine how much they can destroy. That same conviction can provide us, however, with a freedom to look with steady eye at the path marked out for us by God through his servant Jesus and to walk it with boldness, courage, and humility.

Above all, my pattern of presentation tries to place at the center a Christ who was sent by God to love his enemies and to teach his disciples to love their enemies; a Christ who was God's act of vengeance against a disobedient world thus ending once and for all the need for human vengeance, and above all, a Christ who is therefore our peace. That same Jesus came into history and partook of a culture and a society which had been prepared for what he said and what he did. For this reason we appreciate Jesus more as we look carefully at the Greeks and Romans, as well as Jesus' Jewish contemporaries from whom he derived his basic theological and ethical position.

If perchance there are those who think what is contained herein is so radical that in fact it is a threat to peace rather than contributing to it, I must reply with the words from the *Tanhuma Mishpatim:*

> If a man of learning participates in public affairs . . . he gives stability to the land. But if he sits in his home and says to himself, "What have the affairs of society to do with me? . . . Why should I trouble myself with

the people's voices of protest? Let my soul dwell in peace!"—If he does this, he destroys the world.[7]

NOTES

1. Quoted from the wire copy of excerpts issued by the White House on March 9, 1983.

2. In *Dear Bess,* ed. Robert H. Ferrell (New York: W. W. Norton, 1983), 551–52.

3. Thomas R. Berger, *Fragile Freedoms: Human Rights and Dissent in Canada* (Toronto: Clarke, Irwin and Co., 1981), 120, 115 respectively.

4. Anthony Lewis, "If Reagan Claims God, It's Time to Get Nervous," *New York Times,* quoted from the *Vancouver Province,* March 11, 1983.

5. Above all, Peter Craigie, *The Problem of War in the Old Testament* (Grand Rapids: Wm. B. Eerdmans, 1978). Also see Millard Lind, *Yahweh as Warrior* (Scottdale, Pa.: Herald Press, 1980); Patrick D. Miller, *The Divine Warrior in Early Israel* (Cambridge: Harvard Univ. Press, 1973); and Waldemar Janzen, "The Burden of War," in *Still in His Image: Essays in Biblical Theology and Anthropology* (Newton, Kans.: Faith and Life Press, 1982), 173–211.

6. See Tom Cornell, "The Catholic Church and Witness Against War," in *War or Peace? The Search for New Answers,* ed. Thomas A. Shannon (Maryknoll, N.Y.: Orbis Books, 1980), 200–213. Much of the impetus given to this movement came from Dorothy Day (see William Miller's *Dorothy Day: A Biography* [New York: Harper & Row, 1982]).

7. Quoted from John Ferguson, *War and Peace in the World's Religions* (New York and London: Oxford Univ. Press, 1978), 95.

CHAPTER 1

Peace and Victory
Over the Enemy
in Greek Thought

In the earliest history of human life vengeance is considered a normal response to injury.[1] It is also the greatest single cause of war. There has been much debate over the question whether humans have an innate tendency towards violence or if it is a trait which gradually emerged over the centuries.[2] The earliest human remains discovered seem to bear the marks of violent murder; nevertheless, some people argue that primitive humans were peace-loving.

Whatever its origins, it is clear that violence has been universally adopted by humans in a way that other animals have not. While ants may make war on each other, there is surely nothing in the animal kingdom comparable to what Hitler did to the Jews, or the Allies did to Dresden, or the destruction the Americans visited on Hiroshima and more recently on Indo-China.

In this survey we trace the development of folk or common sense morality in pre-Socratic Greece on the question of vengeance in particular. In doing so, both the commitment to peace and its union with the idea of loving your enemies become visible.[3]

THE GREEK POETS AND VENGEANCE:
EMERGING CONSENSUS

In the earliest Greek epic poems, the *Iliad* and the *Odyssey,* there are passages which indicate an unrelenting thirst for vengeance. Compassion is also revealed in several instances. These passages appear to reflect not only the "military mind" of that period but also the thinking of the common people who were influenced by such a mentality. Since the *Iliad* and the *Odyssey* are war poems, it is natural that their conception of life would reflect a time of conflict.

Some of the passages in the *Iliad* indicate that escalating violence was considered the central element in man's conduct. One instance is the episode in which Menelaus, the Greek, has conquered the Trojan, Adrastus, and is about to slay him. Menelaus is inclined to accede to the young man's plea for his life when Agamemnon, commander of the expeditionary corps, arrives and without hesitation kills Adrastus and says:

> No; we are not going to leave a single one of them alive, down to the babies in their mothers' wombs—not even they must live. The whole people must be wiped out of existence, and none be left to think of them and shed a tear (*Iliad* VI.57–60).

Although the *Odyssey* has a milder attitude toward violence, at one point it sees forgiveness of an enemy as an insult to the memory of the dead who have fallen in the war:

> The disgrace of it will echo down the generations should we fail to punish the murderer of our sons and kindred (*Odyssey* XXIV.433–34).

The theme which is heard in every war, that the enemy is not "normal," is also spoken by Menelaus: "But these Trojans are not normal men; they are gluttons for war" (*Iliad* XII.636).

Voices are raised centuries later to halt the relentless desire for brutality and revenge. Words from Sophocles' (496–406 B.C.E.) *Ajax* call attention to the fact that even the foe's destiny is tied to one's own, for in the evil fate which encompasses him we see our own humanity. All who live are, after all, but "phantom forms, shadows without essence" (125–26). Pindar (522–443 B.C.E.) likewise urges that "be a man friend or foe, let him not hide good work that is done for the common weal, and thus do wrong to the precept of the old man of the sea, who bade us give praise that is hearty and fair, even to one's foe" (*Pythian Ode* IX.92–95).

There is at least one incident in the *Iliad* in which Athena intervenes to stay Achilles' anger against Agamemnon. Sent by the goddess Hera, "who loves you both equally in her heart and cares for you," Athena is quite aware of the outrage done to Achilles but bids him not to take sword in hand, "keep clear of fighting, though indeed with words you may abuse him." She promises that he will be rewarded threefold, and he agrees since he looks forward to continuing favours from the gods (*Iliad* I.185–215).

All three of the major tragic poets, Aeschylus (524–436 B.C.E.), Sophocles (496–406 B.C.E.), and Euripides (480–406 B.C.E.) protest explicitly against the senselessness and futility of war and the pain that violence causes. Yet, the deep roots which the desire for vengeance has in human nature are given full play even while the costs to the human spirit of hatred towards an enemy are graphically portrayed. The most important point, made especially by Euripides, seems to be that the gods cannot be blamed for human violence and that enemies are made by humans, not provided by the deities. All of the tragic poets are able to see that a role reversal can take place, and that our own fate may be inextricably bound to the fate of the enemy. In this insight lies the seed for a more creative approach to human conflict.

Once the possibility exists of putting oneself into the place of the other and playing that role, many opportunities present themselves. "The enemy can be seen to possess nobility, and the self can be regarded from the standpoint of its critics."[4] Eventually out of such experiences comes the abandonment of retaliation and the rule of Isocrates which approaches the golden rule: "Do not do to others that which angers you when they do it to you."[5] "You should be such in your dealings with others as you expect me to be in my dealings with you."[6]

Although Euripides states that common folk morality, "Son, worthy of thee it is to love your friends, to hate your foes," he also adds, "yet be not over–rash" (*Madness of Hercules,* 585–586). Throughout the writings of this great artist runs the strain that human violence leads to great pain and suffering. Euripides was the first to point to the incredible human suffering that comes when people indulge themselves in the "pleasure" of revenge and retaliation, when violence is glorified.

As an artist, Euripides not only struck out against the old art forms by creating new forms but also stood as an articulate dissenter from the way his contemporaries saw the role of the deities in history. Above all he attacked their glorification of vengeance and of war.[7] He did so by showing what an enormous price humans paid for all forms of violence, especially those sanctioned by society. According to A. Gouldner, Euripides leads a "savage assault upon the heroic tradition," but it "is only the core of a larger attack upon a compulsive conformity with any of the conventional virtues that is mindless of human costs." Euripides rejects the ancient code of reciprocity and as against manly physical courage: "it is love he extols as the vital source of the strength needed to cope with the senseless suffering to which humans are subjected: 'For love is all we have, the only way that each can help the other.' "8

Nevertheless in the total Greek poetic literature the theme of rejoicing over the enemy occurs so often that one scholar correctly concludes:

> Everywhere hatred of one's enemy and revenge are not only considered permissible but commanded and demanded . . . There is hardly any other teaching which is expressed so often and is so widely in evidence.9

A break with this consensus is first seen in the writings of the historians who do not hesitate to select their material and interpret it in such a way as to influence their readers against such an exaltation of violence.

Preparatory work for the break had been done by the comedians, in particular by Aristophanes in three of his eleven extant comedies in which he addresses himself to ending the Peloponnesian War. *The Acharnians* (425 B.C.E.) is written to strengthen the hands of the peace party at Athens. In it, Dicaeopolis, an honest countryman, decides to pursue peace singlehandedly in opposition to the angry vengeful men of Acharnae. In return he receives the blessings of life while Lamachus, leader of the war party, smarts from cold, wounds, and snow. *The Peace* (421 B.C.E.), advocating peace with Sparta, played at the Great Dionysia just before the conclusion of the peace treaty. It portrays Trygaeus, a distressed Athenian soaring to the sky on a dung-beetle's back. There the gods (of war) are pounding to death the various Greek states in a mortar. In order to put an end to the destruction, Trygaeus must rescue Eirēnē, the goddess imprisoned in a well. When he does so, the gods lay aside the mortar and pestle. Trygaeus marries one of the handmaids of Peace, and the countryside is restored again to prosperity.

Reference should be made as well to Aristophanes' play, *Lysistrata,* where the Athenian women stage the first sit-in in history by occupying the Parthenon, the temple where the war-chest is housed. They aim at protecting human values by putting an end to barbarous devastation. The women refuse love in a protest against war and seek thereby to restore their society to a deeper appreciation of love. Undoubtedly audiences chuckled as it was portrayed in Athens, but they also must have been able to see the deeper meaning of it as well.[10]

Aristophanes cleverly debunked life as it was. He lacked the intellect to portray what could be in its place. It is going too far to describe him as a pacifist. But his call, "Tis now the moment when freed of quarrels and fighting, we should rescue sweet Peace and draw her out of this pit, before some other pestle prevents us," issued to all members of his society is as timely today as it was twenty-four hundred years ago.[11]

THE GREEK HISTORIANS

Herodotus of Halicarnassus (484–425 B.C.E.) reveals a profound distaste for war and refuses to exalt the wars of the past. "No man is so foolish as to desire war more than peace: for in peace, sons bury their fathers, but in war fathers bury their sons" (*History* I.87). War is monstrous, especially when it was waged between members of the same country. He saw it as the "lowest form of human conduct, the consequence of a state of madness."[12] His pessimism about human nature is too profound for him to emerge with anything that could transcend the complexity of human enmity.

Thucydides (455–400 B.C.E.), who belonged to the succeeding generation, while reflecting the common folk morality also transcends it.

The most unusual transcendence of the general maxim, "to be hard on one's enemies," appears in the speech of the Spartan peace mission of 425 B.C.E. recorded by Thucydides. In asking for the release of the men blockaded on Sphacteria, the messengers present a variation of the theory of friendship which Pericles had elaborated in the funeral Oration:

> The Lacedaemonians therefore invite you to accept terms and bring the war to an end. . . . We believe, too, that a permanent reconciliation of bitter enmities is more likely to be secured, not when one party seeks revenge and, because he has gained a decided mastery in the war, tries to

bind his opponent by compulsory oaths and thus makes peace with him on unequal terms, but when, having it in his power to secure the same result by clemency, he vanquishes his foe by generosity also, offering him terms of reconciliation which are moderate beyond all his expectations. For the adversary, finding himself now under obligation to repay the generosity in kind, instead of striving for vengeance for having had terms forced upon him, is moved by a sense of honor and is more ready to abide by his agreements. (*History* IV.xix.1–3).

The fundamental affirmations of a better approach to human conflict are all here: the appeal is to generosity and clemency as springing not from weakness but from strength. Revenge has to give place to a sincere desire for reconciliation, although the contest terminology is retained, for "he vanquishes his foe by generosity." Finally, it is affirmed that the best hopes for future peace lie in such an approach, for the whole scheme is built upon a person's sense of honour. The appeal went unheeded with tragic consequences for all antagonists.[13]

DISSOLUTION OF THE CONSENSUS

The gnomic poets and ethical teachers were the first to break with the consensus on hating the enemy and loving your friends.

Plato cites the maxim that the friend is to be helped and the enemy to be harmed, as accepted by the majority *(doxa tōn pollōn)*. Its force in Greek society stands evident. As A. Dihle has shown, it was particularly valued by the Greek nobility of the beginning period[14] and was based to a large extent on the principle of reciprocity as well as the high place which honor *(timē)* held. Saving face was of primary importance among Homeric nobility. The man who refused to defend his own or himself was considered a shameful man without gall.[15]

The severest attack against this consensus was led by Socrates and Plato. To the Socratic Plato belongs the credit for the radical overthrow. Gradual approaches to its overthrow were made, however, by others. Pythagoras (582–500 B.C.E.) taught his followers "so to behave one to another as not to make friends into enemies but to turn enemies into friends."[16] He built a community on the idea that enemies could be turned into friends. In this formula the traditional is turned on its head, and the maxim is given a creative twist in which the state of enmity is not absolutized or seen as static but open to change.

Democritus of Abdera's (460–370 B.C.E.) dictum that "whoever does an injustice is worse than the one who endures one," (45) was important to Socrates as was his insight that not only the act but also the intention is important, for the "enemy is not one who does wrong but who wishes to do so" (89).

Democritus does not ignore enmity and specifically warns that when good deeds are done one should "beware that the recipient does not repay you evil instead of good" (93), and the "bad man should be watched lest he take advantage of his opportunity" (87). Nevertheless, his conclusion on strife is: "Every lust for strife is stupid; for by concentrating on the ill of the enemy it loses sight of one's own advantage" (237). He appeals to enlightened self-interest in dealing with the enemy and even transcends the traditional motives for doing good when he says: "Doing good is not looking to the results, but wishing to do it out of free initiative" (96).[17]

The position of Democritus runs counter to the grain of Greek folk morality. Socrates assured him a place of creative importance in the replacement of the maxim to hate or hurt one's enemies.

One further fact which contributed to the dissolution of the maxim was the emerging idea of the cosmopolis. Democritus said, "To the wise man every land is open; for the whole world is the native country of a good soul" (247). Although the concept of human unity awaited later development, the Stoic notion of kinship *(oikeiotēs)* defined by Plutarch as "the perception and apprehension of what is akin to oneself" *(SVF* II.724) also opened the way for a more humane approach to one's fellow, even an enemy. The idea reaches its furthest extreme in the words of Aristippus of Cyrene (435–356 B.C.E.) who replied to Socrates' argument that those who seek another lot than rule or subjection are only crushed by the strong: "Well, for my part, to avoid suffering this fate, I do not shut myself up within the confines of a state, but am a stranger everywhere" (Xenophon, *Memorabilia* II.i.13).[18] As the idea of the unity of the human race emerged and gained general acceptance about the first-century B.C., this seed bore fruit.

There are, moreover, several anecdotes which also point to a better way. Seen against this background of folk morality, the noble behavior of Lycurgus of Lacedaemonia stands out. According to legend, during a riot in Sparta, Lycurgus fled from his house only to be apprehended by a certain Alcander who pierced his one eye with a stick. Later, when Lycurgus was granted the privilege to get even with his enemy as he wished, he received Alcander affectionately into his home, allowed him to share his daily food, and to live with him, thus establishing an enduring friendship with him.[19]

There is also the well-known legend of Aristides, son of Lysimachus of Athens, who admired and sought to emulate Lycurgus.[20] Plutarch (50–120 C.E.) says that just as "kings," "conquerors," and some "eagles" or "hawks," cultivated a reputation based on violence and power, so Aristides acquired the surname "the Just." At first he was loved for this surname but later on he was jealously hated, which led to his ostracism. The procedure was that each voter took an *ostrakon* (potsherd) and wrote on it the name of the citizen whom he wished to have removed from the city. Plutarch continues:

> Now at the time of which I was speaking, as the voters were inscribing their *ostraka*, it is said that an unlettered and utterly boorish fellow handed his *ostrakon* to Aristides, whom he took to be one of the ordinary crowd, and asked him to write *Aristides* on it. He, astonished, asked the man what possible wrong Aristides had done him. "None whatever," was the answer, "I don't even know the fellow, but I am tired of hearing him everywhere called 'The Just'." On hearing this, Aristides made no answer, but wrote his name on the *ostrakon* and handed it back.[21]

As Aristides left the city, he lifted up his hands to heaven and prayed that no crisis might overtake the Athenians which would compel them to remember Aristides.[22]

The kindness of Pittacus of Mitylene (c.a. 600 B.C.E.) towards the smith who killed his son with an axe while he was in a barber shop in Cyme, is also reported by several writers. When the people of Cyme sent the murderer to Pittacus, "he, on learning the story, set him at liberty and declared that 'It is better to pardon now than to repent later' *(Syngnomē metanoias kreisson)*." According to Heraclitus he had freed another man who was in his power with the words, "Mercy is better than vengeance" *(syngnomē timorias kreisson)*. The same man is credited with the maxim: "Speak no ill of a friend, nor even of an enemy."[23]

Early and universal as the interest in retaliation appears to be, the desire to go beyond it is also early. Thus, Pindar in his earliest datable poem lauds the blessed life of the Hyperboreans who know not war and strife and do not live under the law of retaliation (*Pythian Ode* X.43). According to A. Dihle, the gradual transcendence of the law of retaliation was motivated by the following factors:

1. The recognition that since exact retaliation cannot usually be carried out, but more importantly because one cannot foresee the consequences of retaliation and determine the chain of reactions which follow, it is more advantageous, wiser, and also morally better to respond with forgiveness and to answer an evil deed with a deed of kindness.

The idea that forgiveness is better than vengeance is found among the sayings of the so-called seven wise men,[24] as well as in the story told of Pittacus by Diogenes Laertius (*Lives* I.76). The same writer reports that when Antisthenes heard that Plato spoke ill of him he replied: "It is a royal privilege to do good and be ill spoken of."[25]

The model of *epieikēs,* the ability to make allowances, is already applied before the breakthrough of philosophical ethics. An episode in Herodotus illustrates this. The daughter of Periander, the Corinthian tyrant, expressed the opinion that her brother had best refrain from the retaliation which is his due and based her opinion on the generally accepted view that *epieikēs* has the advantage over the *dikaion* (the just).[26] This is an early instance in Greek literature of the widespread idea which later replaced formal justice with *epieikēs*: making allowances. The simple consideration of special circumstances, basic good will toward the other, the curbing of one's own rights, all of these are seen in the light of *epieikeia.*

2. Another motivation is the deepening reflection about the nature of the human from which all actions arise. Motivation and intentions are considered, and this leads to an assessment of an action in a different key. Democritus especially led in this approach, and eventually he concluded that doing wrong is worse than enduring it. In biblical ethics it led to the conclusion that since only God knows heart and mind, the question of retaliation must also be left in his hands.

3. A third factor is the emergence of doubt about the rightness of one's own position. Is it not possible that in assuming one is wronged and in committing an act of retaliation, one in turn commits an act of sacrilege? The conclusion emerges that only seldom can one be sure that one is in the right and the enemy is in the wrong. Human fate is

after all not in our own hands, and the giver and receiver may change places tomorrow. In the capricious changes of fate it was increasingly seen that the basis for retaliation was too slender to justify a harsh approach. The Greek tragedies taught a basic respect for the other person, and the automatic equation of deed and retaliation had to give in to a deeper understanding of a person's relationship to one's fellows. Thus it emerged that a person could meet one's fellow human being with respect and good will and not seek to repay evil for evil.

All of these themes are brought together in the speech of Nicolaus, reported by Diodorus Siculus in his *History* (XIII. 19–27). Writing in the late-first-century B.C.E. he constructs a speech which appeals to the men of Syracuse to be lenient with the captives they have taken from Athens.

The old man, Nicolaus, had himself lost two sons in the war and only because of that was afforded a hearing. He appeals to reason and to their humanity. He points out that Cyrus became king over all of Asia "by his considerate treatment of the conquered" and became, in fact, their benefactor. He appeals to his countrymen "to surpass the Athenians not only in feats of arms but also in humanity." Twice he uses the verb to "overcome" *(nikaō)* the Athenians in philanthropy or with kindness. Like Thucydides there is the note of "overcoming the enemy" with kindness. He urges also that they should not lose sight of the accomplishments of the Greeks: "Brief is the hatred aroused by the wrong they have committed, but important and many are their accomplishments which claim goodwill" (27.2). As a historian Diodorus is not to be trusted, but as one who expressed his own values with respect to how enemies are to be treated if one is to prevent one war from leading to another, he is an important source.

The essential overthrow of the consensus on the philosophical level was not accomplished before Plato.[27] Nevertheless, the seeds for this were sown long before his time. With the figure of Socrates, Plato undertook to overturn at its roots the idea of retaliation and vengeance.

Socrates refused to accept the notion that it is best to harm your enemies and do good to your friends. Not only was he the first philosophically to challenge this commonplace notion, but he also undergirded his teaching with his example. He argued that by returning evil for evil, one participates in evil, but by refraining from doing so he affirms his conviction that an evil man cannot hurt a good person: "for I am sure that God will not allow a good man to be injured by a bad one" (*Apology* 30D). He realized that only a few people would ever hold that opinion (*Crito* 49D).

The influence of Socrates for the first century can be seen in at least three aspects. When Plutarch records Cleomenes' advice to a king "To do good to one's friends and evil to one's enemies," he states that when it was commended to Ariston, King of Sparta (560–510 B.C.E.), he replied: "How much better, my good sir, to do good to friends and to make friends of our enemies." Plutarch adds that it is a maxim universally attributed to Socrates.[28]

Furthermore, in Plato's portrait of the suffering of the just man he says that such a person

> . . . will have to endure the lash, the rack, chains, the branding iron in his eyes, and finally after every extremity of suffering, he will be crucified, and so will learn his lesson that not to be but to seem just is what we ought to desire. (*Republic* 362A)

Plato knew that those who live by this new concept of justice will not only be in the minority but can also expect rejection by others. To be popular one has to *seem* just, not *be* just—a statement which appears to reflect Socratic irony. Although there are differences, the central affirmation has affinities with Isaiah's suffering servant and the New Testament's interest in Jesus: the just man suffering for the sins of others.[29]

Finally, the strongest evidence of Socrates' influence in the first century can be seen in the life of Musonius Rufus (30–101 C.E.), called the "Roman Socrates." It is to Socrates that he appeals in his discussion that exile is not really an evil: "Tell me, is not the universe the common fatherland of all men, as Socrates held?"(ix).

The most extensive use of Socrates comes, however, when Musonius deals with the question of returning evil for evil. The wise man, Musonius argues, does not think that disgrace lies in enduring blows but rather in giving them. Clearly this is an application of Socrates' ideas seen above. Socrates did not defend his rights or revile when he was reviled or retaliate when violence or bodily harm was done to him. Musonius says that he could mention many other men who have not defended their rights against their assailants "but very meekly bore their wrong." He continues (x):

> And in this they were quite right. For to scheme how to bite back the biter and to return evil for evil is the act not of a human being but of a wild beast, which is incapable of reasoning. . . . But to accept injury not in a spirit of savage resentment and to show ourselves not implacable toward those who wrong us, but rather be a source of good hope to them is a characteristic of a benevolent and civilised way of life.

The last sentence is a rather remarkable affirmation. Musonius seems to say that to accept injury in this manner is not only good for the person doing it but also is the way in which the enemy can find a way out of his own situation. It offers him a way of escape from the state of enmity. The philosopher cuts a much better figure when "he deems worthy of forgiveness anyone who wrongs him" (x) than if he rushes to the courts to insist on his rights.[30]

Paul must have addressed people who had also been exposed to these ideas, and although there were profound differences between Paul and Musonius, the appeals to imitate Socrates found among the educated population would have made them receptive to the invitation to imitate or follow Jesus. On this fundamental question of human existence, whether you retaliate when abused or attacked or whether you endure the suffering inflicted upon you, Jesus and Socrates agreed.

Gregory Vlastos draws the contrast in this way. He attributes Socrates' failure not to knowledge but to a failure of love. "Jesus wept for Jerusalem. Socrates warns Athens, scolds, exhorts it, condemns it. But he has no tears for it."[31] Nevertheless there remains in the legacy of Socrates a great victory. Not only did he stress the human dimension and the need for human knowledge to rule over passion, he also challenged one of the most fundamental and pervasive myths of his time and ours. With right Vlastos asks:

> How many practices or sentiments in Socrates' world or ours would remain intact if his conviction that it is never right to return evil for evil were taken seriously as really true?[32]

NOTES

1. Among the older treatments, cf. M. Waldmann, *Die Feindesliebe* (Vienna: Mayer, 1902), 19–41; E. Bach, *Die Feindesliebe* (Kempton:

Kösel'schen, 1914), 6–26; S. Randlinger, *Die Feindesliebe* (Paderborn: Schöningh, 1906), 32–83; F. Steinmüller, *Die Feindesliebe* (Regensburg, 1909), 17–26. The best recent one is by A. Dihle, *Die Goldene Regel* (Göttingen: Vandenhoeck & Ruprecht, 1962), 13–41.

2. See Robert Bigelow, *The Dawn Warriors: Man's Revolution Toward Peace* (Boston: Little, Brown, 1969).

3. See G. Zampaglione, *The Idea of Peace in Antiquity,* ET: Richard Dunn (Notre Dame, Ind.: Notre Dame Univ. Press, 1973), 18–23.

4. A. Gouldner, *The Hellenic World* (New York: Harper & Row, 1969), 114.

5. Isocrates, *Nicocles or the Cyprians* 61. Cf. *To Demonicus* 14; *To Nicocles* 24, 38; *Panegyricus* 81.

6. Isocrates, *Nicocles or the Cyprians* 49; cf. 62. See A. Dihle, *Die Goldene Regel* 51–60, 85–95.

7. One thinks in particular of the plays *Medea* and *Women of Troy* and the impact of Jean-Paul Sartre's version of the latter on New York audiences during the American war against Vietnam.

8. Euripides, *Orestes* iv.209, 298–99. Gouldner, *Hellenic World,* 112. See also G. Murray, *Euripides* (London: Oxford Univ. Press, 1965), 4–5.

9. F. Nägelsbach, as cited by Waldmann, *Die Feindesliebe,* 24. See also Dihle, *Die Goldene Regel,* 31–40. L. Schmidt, *Die Ethik der alten Griechen* (Berlin: Hertz, 1882), II: 355: "The Greeks were as deeply enslaved to enmity as they were devoted to friendship."

10. See the superb work by David Daube in *Civil Disobedience in Antiquity* (Edinburgh: Edinburgh Univ. Press, 1972), 17–22.

11. H. Sharpley, *The Peace of Aristophanes,* edited with a commentary (Edinburgh: Wm. Blackwood, 1905), 294–99.

12. Zampaglione, *Idea of Peace,* 91–92.

13. See Lionel Pearson, "Popular Ethics in the World of Thucydides," *Classical Philology* 52 (1957): 228–44, esp. 234–35.

14. Dihle, *Die Goldene Regel,* 32–33. The general acceptance of vengeance and repaying evil with evil is expressed pithily by Sophocles:

Heaven's justice never smites
Him who ill with ill requites
(*Oedipus at Colonus,* 231–32).

15. The maxim is not restricted to the nobility however. Dihle (*ibid.*, 33) finds it in Hesiod (*Works and Days,* 353–54), Euripides (*Madness of Hercules,* 585–86, 732–33; *Medea* 809; *Ion* 1046; *Hecuba* 1250), the Socrates of Xenophon (*Memorabilia* II.ii.14; II.vi.24) and the definitions of *virtus* of the first-century writer Lucilius (1326–27) in F. Marx, *C. Lucili Carminum Reliquiae* (Leipzig: Teubner, 1904).

16. According to Diogenes Laertius, *Lives of Eminent Philosophers* VIII.23. See Zampaglione, *Idea of Peace,* 35–37. Pythagoras was a contemporary of Heraclitus who described war as the "father of all things, the King

of all" (B53) and praised it for "drawing people together and justice is strife; and all life originates through strife and necessity" (B80). See Bruno Snell, *Heraklit: Fragmente* (Munich: Heimeran, 1976).

17. Sayings of Democritus, in H. Diels and W. Kranz, *Fragmente der Vorsokratiker,* 6th rev. ed. (Zurich and Dublin: Weidmann, 1968), au. trans.

18. See H. C. Baldry, *The Unity of Mankind in Greek Thought* (Cambridge: Cambridge Univ. Press, 1965), 58–61, whose translation I follow here.

19. The legend has many variations. Plutarch reports in the *Lives* that after the youth had moved to Lycurgus' dwelling the latter did him no harm by word or deed.

> Abiding thus with Lycurgus, and sharing his daily life, he came to know the gentleness *(praotēta)* of the man, the calmness of his spirit, the rigid simplicity of his habits, and his unwearied industry. He thus became a devoted follower of Lycurgus and used to tell his intimates and friends that the man was not harsh nor self-willed, as he had supposed, but the mildest and gentlest *(hemeros kai praos)* of them all. Such, then, was the chastisement *(ekekolasto)* of this young man, and such the penalty *(dikēn)* laid upon him, namely to become, instead of a wild and impetuous youth, a most decorous and discreet man *(Lycurgus* XI.3–4).

King Charilaüs also described as having a "gentle disposition" *(physei praos ōn)* raises a problem for his royal colleague Archelaus: "How can Charilaüs be a good man, when he has no severity even for the bad?" *(Lycurgus* V.5)

20. Plutarch, *Aristides* II.1.

21. Plutarch, *Aristides* VII.6.

22. Plutarch (ibid.) observes that the prayer seems to be the opposite to that which Achilles made "to pen them in among the sterns of their ships and around the sea as they are slain." *(Iliad* I.409). Aristides prays on behalf of his enemies.

23. Diogenes Laertius, *Lives* I.76.

24. Dihle, *Die Goldene Regel,* 45, who cites Cheilon according to Diodorus Siculus, *History* 9.9.3–4.

25. *basilikon kalōs poiounta kakōs akouein* (VI.4). Cf. also Plutarch, *Alexander* XLI; *Antony* XXXVI.

26. Diodorus Siculus, *History* 3.53.4.

27. It is fallacious however to assume that war was seen as preferred to peace in the ancient world. Wilhelm Nestle *(Der Friedensgedanke in der antiken Welt* [Leipzig: Dietrich'sche, 1938]) has demonstrated how persistent the thought is that peace is the better way and cites Gorgias's (fifth century B.C.E.) equation: peace is health, war is disease. He rejects the notion that war is the normal state of things in antiquity although concedes that war is not rejected fundamentally (p. 75). He concludes his book, published in those ominous times, with the sober reminder that Christianity did not alter the course of history with respect to war. If anything "the christian nations have

butchered each other in no less gruesome a manner during the middle ages and in modern times than did the pagans of antiquity—indeed they shamefully added an ingredient missing totally in antiquity, namely the concept of the religious war" (p. 76).

28. Plutarch, *Sayings of Spartans* 218. The LCL editor, F. C. Babbitt (*Moralia*, LCL III) notes that it does not appear in these precise words in the Platonic dialogues (*Republic* 335B–E; *Crito* 48E–49E; *Gorgias* 469A–B, 475B–D). Diogenes Laertius attributes a similar comment to Cleobulus (*Lives* I.91).

29. Romano Guardini, *The Death of Socrates* (Cleveland and New York: World Pub., 1962), V. Guardini's work and that of Ernst Benz (*Der gekreuzigte Gerechte bei Plato, im Neuen Testament und in der alten Kirche* [Wiesbaden: Steiner, 1950]) first led me to give serious consideration to Socrates in connection with this study. See also among an abundance of literature, James Beckman, *The Religious Dimension of Socrates' Thought* (Waterloo: Wilfrid Laurier Univ. Press, 1979); Erich Fascher, "Sokrates und Christus," *ZNW* 45 (1945): 1–41; H. Hommel, im "Herrenworte in Lichte sokratischer Überlieferung," *ZNW* 47 (1956): 1–27.

30. Translations of Musonius Rufus by Cora Lutz in *Yale Classical Studies* 10 (1947): 33–145; for commentary see W. Klassen, "Humanitas" *Studi Storico Religiosi* 1 (1977): 63–82.

31. G. Vlastos, ed. *The Philosophy of Socrates* (Garden City, N.Y.: Doubleday & Co., 1971), 16.

32. Ibid., 18–19. Matthew Melko and Richard D. Weigel (*Peace in the Ancient World* [Jefferson, N.C.: McFarland, 1981], 158–69) have shown that the ancient world knew long periods of peace in various major geographical areas. The values that made it possible according to them were: tolerance, commitment to justice, placing a high value on the human, and especially seeing peace as a laudable goal.

CHAPTER 2

Love Your Enemy
and Peace in
the Hebrew Bible

The literary sources known collectively as the Old Testament are important for our study, for they form the canon of both the Jewish and the Christian religions. Since for both, ethics[1] are important and neighborly love a central aspect of the devout life, it is of great importance to ask what these sources say about our topic.

The approach pioneered by Marcion in the second century was to consider the Old Testament antiquated because, according to him, it heralded a God of vengeance, while the New Testament proclaimed a God of love. Sixty years ago the famous church historian, Adolf von Harnack, exalted Marcion as exemplary in his approach.[2] Although many Christian scholars betray traces of Marcionite influence, his greatest influence is seen not among scholars but among the rank and file Christians. The approach of Marcion is decisively rejected here because the New Testament writers all follow Jesus in affirming that indissoluble stitches bind together the "old" covenant and the "new" covenants. The God of the Fathers, of Moses, and the prophets is the same as the God of Jesus and of Paul.

Our study, therefore, of the Old Testament is unavoidably complicated by this theological dimension. There is a further complication in the dating of the sources and the various traditions and their interdependence. Every effort has been made to follow the most reliable scholarship. It seemed essential, however, to deal with the materials in the Old Testament even when the treatment does not satisfy the critical eye of the specialist in Old Testament studies, especially since Christian scholars have so often used the Old Testament sources to justify hating and killing the enemy.[3]

The commandment, "love your enemy," occurs nowhere in the Old Testament. The concept, however, cannot be confined to the words themselves. When enemies are fed and cared for, rather than killed or mistreated, then in effect love for the enemy is being practiced. Peace—*shalom*—is a very important idea for the Hebrews, and one cannot understand Jesus or Paul without recognizing that link. We begin with one great threat to peace: The desire for vengeance.

VENGEANCE IN THE OLD TESTAMENT[4]

The Blood Feud and Human Concord

One of the social characteristics of early Israel was the primitive desert institution of vengeance. The Old Testament sources unanimously forbid personal revenge and retaliation against the neighbor, even though the same sources do not explicitly command loving the enemy.[5]

The form in which this issue seems to arise in the narratives is a feud between brothers: Cain and Abel (Genesis 4), Joseph and his brothers (Genesis 37—50), and, especially significant from a theological point of view, the conflict between Jacob and Esau and their reconciliation (Genesis 27—33). There is one important conflict between the appointed king (David) and the king who had lost his charisma (Saul). While not depicted as a classical case of usurpation, one can see it as such. The vengeance motif is introduced there in order to highlight a better way.

The realism of the biblical narratives comes to expression in the fact that the first parents produced a murderer. Although efforts are made to dissuade Cain from murdering Abel, the fever of his envy increases until it bears fruit in murder. As a result of this murder, the ground is cursed and Cain is no longer able to receive from it the productivity which it originally had (Gen. 4:12). Cain is condemned to the life of a fugitive and wanderer upon the face of the earth. This estrangement from the "ground" is a result of the pollution which it has suffered: human blood. Cain is offered the protection of the Lord, but it is a threat for greater vengeance: "Not so! If anyone slays Cain, vengeance shall be taken on him sevenfold" (4:15). As a sequel to the Cain and Abel narrative stands the Lamech couplet (4:23–24):

I have slain a man for wounding me,
   a young man for striking me.
If Cain is avenged sevenfold,
   truly Lamech seventy-sevenfold.

Not only does the conflict between brothers lead to murder, but the vengeance quotient has moved rapidly from sevenfold to the limitless figure: seventy-sevenfold. In later attempts to restrict vengeance (within biblical history) it is not until Jesus' time that this same figure is applied to forgiveness. Instead of unlimited vengeance, Peter is told that forgiving a brother when he sins against him seven times is not enough, but rather forgiveness seventy times seven is necessary (Matt. 18:22; cf. Luke 17:4 which restricts it to seven times a day).

According to George Mendenhall, it is important for our fuller understanding of vengeance in the Bible that the root *NQM* appears only here (Gen. 4:12) in biblical literature in connection with blood vengeance. He argues that any society which has developed far enough to be able to write accounts of such feuds would also have transcended the blood feud as a socially acceptable means of obtaining redress.[6] According to the point of view of the biblical writers, the blood feud "was characteristic of the period before the Flood and was escalated into intolerability in the famous Song of Lamech."[7]

This primitive song, intoning the braggadocio of retaliation in which a man boasts that he killed a man in return for a wound—a young man in return for a blow—is presented as the obverse side of progress. A profound change in human consciousness has come hand in glove with progress. This spirit of hardening irreconcilability and wild self-assertion tears apart the fabric of human coexistence when vengeance is uncontained. The account forms the climax of a series in which the Fall and the murder which Cain committed lead to man taking to himself a right which clearly does not belong to him: the right to take revenge.

The Yahwist does not draw any moral. The account speaks for itself. The act of the first couple in questioning God is very small indeed compared to that of Lamech. For where they timidly asked and acted as if they had been misinformed, Lamech (Gen. 4:19–24) strides into the inner domain of Yahweh and brags to his wives that he has taken to himself that which belongs only to God.[8] As Eve gloried in her ability to give birth with the help of God, thus in some sense finding an equality with God in that she can bring life into being, so Lamech has made himself equal to God by cutting short the life of a man who merely wounded him.[9]

The Patriarchs

On the whole, the Patriarchs are depicted as men with armies who were able to fight for their land and to protect their women. Abraham shows a gentle and patient side when he intercedes on behalf of the cities of Sodom and Gomorrah (Gen. 18:22–33).

Sibling rivalry began for Jacob and Esau in the womb and reached many levels of trickery and deception. Eventually, these years of deceit and treachery brought a confrontation between Jacob and Esau, which is described masterfully by the narrator (Genesis 33). He used every literary device to heighten the tension, and we are prepared for a clash of armies but it never takes place. Why it did not take place is not clearly stated; perhaps it is because of the new self-awareness that has come to Jacob as he wrestled throughout the night. Perhaps Esau too had experienced a change and was able to meet his brother without hatred or rancor or the desire for revenge. Perhaps it was the unexpected generosity of his brother which gave him clear evidence that the new Jacob was able to give and not just grasp for himself.

The only clue which the narrative itself has is the word of Jacob when he says: "For truly to see your face is like seeing the face of God, with such favor have you received me" (Gen. 33:10). Earlier, Jacob had decided to call the place where he wrestled, Peniel (32:30), because there he had seen God face to face. He had struggled hard and won, but he had been spared a bloody battle with his brother, and the editor links together these two incidents. It is as if he were saying that the face of God can be seen in the face of the reconciled brother. God comes not in the absence of strife but in the reconciliation between brothers.

A similar idea is present in the Joseph narrative. Joseph has been wronged by his brothers, and after the death of their father Jacob, the brothers said, "It may be that Joseph will hate us and pay us back for all the evil which we did to him" (Gen. 50:15). And although it is introduced here for the first time, they maintain that Jacob left a message for Joseph urging him to forgive the brothers' crime and wickedness because they did evil to him. With that they begged: "Forgive the transgression of the servants of the God of your father." After the brothers state that they are his slaves, Joseph replies: "Am I in the place of God? As for you, you meant evil against me; but God meant it for good to bring it about that many people should be kept alive" (Gen. 50:19–20).

The narrator seeks to show that Joseph had overcome hatred toward his enemies and that the feud had been resolved. Joseph refused to put himself into the place of God and become an agent of punitive vengeance[10] especially since what the brothers had intended as harm had in fact, through God's sovereignty, become the good of many people. The perspective of God's purpose in history, therefore, takes precedence over personal discomfort or personal spite. Above the petty agenda of humans stands God's own purpose, and God achieves his goal even when people intend to harm their fellows. The Greek moral teachers argued that the persecutions of an enemy could develop one's character and self-discipline. Later, Plutarch could even argue that enemies were more helpful than friends, for they were at least honest and could be trusted to tell the truth about your weaknesses.[11] But the narrator of the Joseph legend seems to say that God can overrule even the malice of brothers and achieve his purpose. God is sovereign and to take vengeance would be to usurp the place of God.

The Terminology of Vengeance

Few aspects of the Bible have been as seriously misinterpreted and misunderstood as vengeance. Both George Mendenhall and Klaus Koch have challenged traditional points of view. "That which is called the 'vengeance' of Yahweh actually designates those events in human experience that were identified as the exercise of the sovereignty— what the ancient Romans called *imperium*."[12]

Two facts form the foundation upon which the peace and security of the community rest. They are the divine sanction and the content of the obligation which the people have taken upon themselves.

> These are actually the twin pillars upon which the entire Old Testament faith rested as a historical fact which, together with the community of human beings which constituted the twelve tribes (not one), make plausible its existence. Tribal religion was characteristic of the period before Moses and after Nehemiah, but not in the nearly thousand years be-

tween the two, in spite of the near success of the pagan tribalism of the monarchy.[13]

The exercise then of imperial power is designated with the verb *NQM* and finds its primary focus in the conduct of the war and prosecution of the internal criminal.

Within biblical literature Mendenhall has noted that of the seventy-eight passages of the Bible where the root *NQM* occurs, fifty-one involve situations in which the actor is either Yahweh or an agency to which the power to act is specifically delegated in a specific situation. In about 55 percent of the uses, the exercise of the divine *imperium* is identified with an attack upon a foreign population. Nearly 20 percent of the occurrences refer to the exercise of the divine *imperium* against Israel herself or against individuals within the community. Mendenhall concludes that Yahweh is never seen as a tribal god of the ancient Israelites. Yahweh is the legitimate power who calls forth absolute obligations from the religious community. Far from being a projection of national self-interest, his demands sometimes appear to run directly counter to such presumed self-interest.[14]

King David and His Enemies

The confrontation between David and Saul is taken as an illustration of defensive vindication.[15] Saul, the duly anointed king, had been disobedient and the Spirit of the Lord left him (1 Sam. 16:14). As a consequence Samuel is commissioned to install David as the new king. The writer of 1 Samuel describes in detail the numerous confrontations between Saul and David. Since David had been playing the harp for Saul, to help him in periods of depression, he knows very well how ill Saul is. Saul's fits of temper, his jealousy and envy of David, and the power at his disposal all make Saul capable of murder, a fact of which David is keenly aware.

Nevertheless, on two occasions when David had an opportunity preemptively to kill his enemy, he refrains from doing so. Even though urged on by his associates and even though he is aware that he is dealing with a "mad man," David does not yield to the temptation of seeing him as either a mad man or an enemy but sees him still as his sovereign and as God's anointed (1 Sam. 24:4–7a). He cannot lift a finger against him, and when he later confronts Saul he says (1 Sam. 24:12–15):

May the Lord judge between me and you, may the Lord avenge me upon you; but my hand shall not be against you. As the proverb of the ancients says, "Out of the wicked comes forth wickedness"; but my hand shall not be against you. After whom has the king of Israel come out? After whom do you pursue? After a dead dog! After a flea! May the Lord therefore be judge, and give sentence between me and you, and see to it, and plead my cause, and deliver me from your hand.

The grounds for historical skepticism in these narratives do not concern us now. Notable is that at least one writer preserved a tradition about David as one who refused to take the normal road to the throne: to kill the incumbent especially when he shows evidence of derangement and David himself had already been anointed. Instead Saul is overwhelmed that on each occasion David shows love for his enemy and spares his life. Through this act of love, Saul comes to his senses and vows never to harm David again (1 Sam. 26:17–25). David himself rejects the method of killing the king in order to become king himself. Instead he loves his enemy.[16]

Traditionally, references are made to the generosity of David in his dealing with Saul. But this does not get to the fundamental issues at stake here. In part, what is involved is the perception of the will of God. For David's attendants it was clear that they should proceed with the killing of Saul and thus end the conflict between the king-designate and the king-discredited. According to H. W. Hertzberg, "what appears to (them) as the will of God seems to him (David) to be a temptation from which God will 'preserve' him." The narrator clearly sees David as being within his rights but the "decisive factor is that David does not stand upon his rights, but leaves their realization to the Lord."[17] David "precisely by recognizing his opponent's rights truly overcomes his opponent."[18]

After becoming king, David shows the same reluctance to harm Absalom, even though he has been guilty of usurpation. David charges Joab to be lenient with Absalom and spare his life (2 Sam. 18:5), but when David became depressed after Joab had killed Absalom, Joab rebuked him with the words: "You love those who hate you and hate those who love you" (2 Sam. 19:6). David's dilemma is clear to every father.

During the conspiracy of Absalom, David was cursed by Shimei with serious curses. When Abishai asks, "Why should this dead dog curse my lord the king? Let me go over and take off his head," David sees behind it the possibility that Shimei is speaking for God. He responds, "Let him alone, and let him curse; for the Lord has bidden him. It may be that the Lord will look upon my affliction, and that the Lord will repay me with good for this cursing of me today" (2 Sam. 16:9–14). David allowed Shimei to continue to curse and throw dust and stones at him. While David does not return the curse with a blessing, it is clear that he is able to see beyond the person of Shimei to the God who stands behind him. Surely for a king such behavior is extraordinary! After the death of Absalom, when Shimei came to David in repentance, David swore an oath that his life would be spared (2 Sam. 19:16–23). On his deathbed, however, David considers it necessary to remind Solomon to repay Shimei (1 Kings 2:9).[19] Solomon was commended for not having prayed for the life of his enemies (1 Kings 3:9–10; 2 Chron. 1:11).

WISDOM LITERATURE

As a background to our understanding of Jewish wisdom literature, it may be of value to look at some Babylonian and Egyptian wisdom literature which bears on this point.

Since ancient Israel had extensive contact with both Egypt and Babylonia, it is not surprising that the proverbial literature of these countries shows some striking parallels to the materials in Proverbs.

In Babylonian proverbs between 1600 and 1700 B.C.E., there is the following advice:

> When confronted with a dispute, go your way; pay no attention to it.
> Should it be a dispute of your own, extinguish the flame!
> Disputes are a *covered* pit,
> A strong wall that scares away its foes.
> They remember what a man forgets and lay the accusation.
> Do not return evil to the man who disputes with you;
> Requite with kindness your evil-doer,
> Maintain justice to your enemy,
> Smile on your adversary.
> If your ill-wisher is [. . . .,] nurture him.
> Do not set your [mind] on evil.
> . . . [. . . . . .] agreeable [to] the gods.
> Evil [. . . . . .] an abomination [. . . . of] Marduk.
>
> Give food to eat, beer to drink,

Grant what is asked, provide for and honour.
In this a man's god takes pleasure,
It is pleasing to Šamaš, who will repay him with favour.
Do charitable deeds, render service all your days.[20]

Very similar advice is given in the second chapter of the Instruction of Amen-Em-Opet dated about 7th–6th centuries B.C.E.:

He who does evil, the (very) river-bank abandons him,
And his *floodwaters* carry him off.
The north wind comes down that it may end his hour;
It is joined to the tempest;
The thunder is loud, and the crocodiles are wicked.
Thou heated man, how art thou (now)?
He is crying out, and his voice (reaches) to heaven.
O moon, establish his crime (against him)!
So steer that we may bring the wicked man across,
For we shall not act like him—
Lift him up, give him thy hand;
Leave him (in) the arms of the god;
Fill his belly with bread of thine,
So that he may be sated and may *be ashamed.*[21]

An Akkadian fragment (prior to 700 B.C.E.) gives advice similar to the Babylonian fragment cited earlier. So similar is the advice, in fact, that some relationship must surely exist between the two fragments.

When you see a quarrel, go away without noticing it.
But if it really is your own quarrel, extinguish the flame;
For a quarrel is a *neglect* of what is right,
A protecting wall . . . (for) the nakedness of one's adversary:
Whoever stops it is thinking about the interests of a friend.
Unto your opponent do no evil;
Your evildoer recompense with good;
Unto your enemy let justice [be done].
Unto your oppressor . . .
Let him rejoice over you, . . . return to him.
Let not your heart be induced to do evil.
　　[some lines lost]
Give food to eat, give date wine to drink;
The one begging for alms honor, clothe:
Over this his god rejoices,
This is pleasing unto the god Shamash, he rewards it with
　　good.
Be helpful, do good.[22]

When we look at Prov. 25:21–23 in this light, it becomes clear that the writer of Proverbs is not outlining something new: "If your enemy is hungry, give him bread to eat; and if he is thirsty, give him water to drink" (v. 21). This admonition is strikingly similar to the Babylonian and Egyptian proverbs. What is quite different is the reason which is given: "for you will heap coals of fire on his head, and the Lord will reward you" (v. 22). This text gains in importance for our discussion since Paul quotes it later in Rom. 12:20, and it will receive further treatment in our discussion there. Much labor has been spent in trying to understand this enigmatic sentence. There is first the problem of the meaning of "coals of fire." It seems entirely out of character to assume that the coals of fire are signals of his destruction, for then the writer would be advocating a cruel hoax. The interpretation of this as a burning sense of shame likewise seems difficult even though it has been very popular since Augustine. There appear to be no reasons why the connection of the coals of fire (cf. p. 120) cannot be made with an Egyptian repentance ritual described by Siegfried Morenz.[23] According to one text, carrying burning coals on the head (where they were quite naturally carried in that society) was a sign of a contestant's desire to bring the feud to a conclusion. Accordingly, the coals of fire are a symbol of willingness to come to truce with the opponent. A 1982 German Bible translates it: "Thus you will bring him to change."

The second problem has to do with the meaning of the last line: "and the Lord will *ĕšallem lāk.*" The usual translation has been "will reward you." Klaus Koch has raised some questions about this interpretation. First, he asks about the etymology of the word *šlm* and points out that the root *šlm* means "unmarred, to be complete." Thus the Piel verb form with its causative meaning should be translated "will complete." If indeed it does mean "reward," then it must have arrived at that meaning via the meaning of completion. He rejects the possibility that the root meaning of the word had changed and considers it probable that *šillem* here has its old meaning, "to make complete." Thus God completes the process which has been inaugurated by the one who showed compassion to his enemy. "Jahweh is seen as above man but he does not deal juridically, by measuring and meting out reward and punishment according to a given norm but renders, so to speak the services of a mid-wife, by bringing to full fruition that which man has set into motion."[24]

Whatever may be the precise meaning of this verse, it is clear that the proverb invites the "wise man" to look to the Lord for his action. He makes no prediction that the enemy will thus be transposed into a friend moved by a show of generosity, or that he will make good use of the foodstuffs given to him. They may be the very means of subsistence the enemy needs to destroy you or at least to harass you all the more. The next act comes from the Lord and that is enough. Having done what you know to be right, the rest can be left with the Lord.

The book of Proverbs also urges the reader: "Do not rejoice when your enemy falls, and let not your heart be glad when he stumbles" (24:17). The principle of retaliation is also rejected (24:29).

Early Prophetic Traditions on Feeding the Enemy

The close connection between wisdom circles and the prophets has long been noted. I would see it extending also to the Hebrew historians. One example is the most striking anecdote on feeding the enemy in 2 Kings 6:15–23. Elisha the prophet and his servant discovered a large Syrian army surrounding their city. Knowing the servant was frightened, Elisha prayed that the young man's eyes be opened to see "the mountain full of horses and chariots of fire round about Elisha." As the Syrians began their attack against Elisha, the Lord struck them with blindness. Elisha then led the defeated Syrian troops to Samaria where the King of Israel asked, "Shall I slay them?" Elisha answers (2 Kings 6:22–23):

> You shall not slay them. . . . Set bread and water before them, that they may eat and drink and go to their master. So he prepared for them a great feast; and when they had eaten and drunk, he sent them away, and they went to their master. And the Syrians came no more on raids into the land of Israel.

The point of the story seems to be that the prophet had his own way of coping with the enemy of the land. Although one sees in the tale a struggle between prophet and king, holy war and regular war, it is the most clear example within the folklore of Hebrew society that at a time of war the enemy could be fed and given water to drink and that such a strategy was effective in stopping his raids. Further work needs to be done in analyzing the relationship of these narratives to the political situation of the time and also in pursuing the relationship between the prophets and the wisdom circles.

According to this narrative, the military strategy taken for granted by the king—it follows all rules of their warfare (cf. 1 Kings 20:42; 1 Sam. 15:33; Deut. 20:13)—is here directly contravened by the prophet. "The act . . . stands out . . . like an isolated mountain peak, high above the moral level of those days. Thus by centuries was anticipated the precept of Rom. 12:19–21."[25]

Elisha should not, however, be made into a person who had the consistent reputation of loving his enemies, for in one of the most petulant stories of the Bible he is described as cursing some young men who taunt him for his baldness and are torn up by bears for this misdemeanor (2 Kings 2:23–25). Like his teacher, Elijah, when personally insulted, Elisha cursed and did not bless, and the powers of the prophet were used to destroy enemies when necessary (2 Kings 1:9–17).

We do not know how widespread the influence of Elisha and the schools of the prophets was. The painstaking work of tracing the relationship between the wisdom and prophetic circles is just beginning. What does seem clear is that some of the storytellers of Israel wished to keep alive the stories about Elisha and the varying relationships he had with kings. It is not necessary to attribute any degree of reliability to these stories to become aware that they were saying something about a better approach to an enemy, rather than killing him, even when the enemy was clearly within Israel's power and when all precedents demand that he be killed. It is precisely this looking beyond traditional solutions to ethical problems and the ability to transcend traditional morality which has given the prophets such a prominent place in the Hebrew-Christian tradition.

Benevolence towards enemies comes to expression clearly in the little Book of Jonah. What has absorbed attention is the miracle of the fish. It has been virtually ignored that Nineveh is the traditional enemy of Israel and that the book portrays a struggle between the prophet Jonah, who seeks revenge, and God, who loves the enemy. Jonah cannot accept that action of God but is forced to be God's herald of love to the enemy. Although Jonah confesses that God is "gracious . . . and merciful, slow to anger and abounding in steadfast love" (4:2), he cannot bring himself to accept that God can also love such evil people as the Ninevites. Like the elder brother in the parable of the two sons (Luke 15:11–32), Jonah prefers to pout when God's love is extended to the enemy rather than to join in the celebration. Jonah is consistent in his anger. God is revealed as one who consistently takes pity on the evil city of Nineveh with its "more than a hundred and twenty thousand persons who do not know their right hand from their left, and also much cattle" (4:11). The miracle of this book, which is as hard for us to accept as it was for Jonah, is that even the worst enemy we can imagine is loved by God and can be brought to repentance if a prophet becomes God's messenger of love.

We cannot leave the Old Testament narratives without referring to the practice, prescribed by certain codes, of annihilating all of Israel's enemies and refusing to make peace with them (e.g., Deut. 23:6). These codes have their place as a desperate plan to maintain the identity of the Israelites against pagan religions. To cite them as normative is, however, to do a grave injustice to the totality of the Hebrew faith. Later interpreters have not seen them as normative but rather as exceptional regulations. In our day we can see the codes as aberrations which came from weakness and failed to draw upon that faith in Yahweh which is the cornerstone of Hebrew faith. Clearly, the great prophets like Isaiah, Jeremiah, and Amos saw the matter in a broader and more humanitarian light. Judaism as a whole, as we shall see in the next chapter, saw that peace could be best maintained when the Jews affirmed God's sovereignty over all mankind. Others were entitled to the same right they expected and deserved: to be allowed to live freely under Yahweh as their sovereign redeemer.[26]

As the prophet Micah states it: "All peoples walk, each in the name of its god, but we will walk in the name of the Lord our God for ever and ever" (4:5). That same prophet struggles to reconcile these two sides of Israel's hope: the desire to be avenged of all the evil the nations have massed against them (4:11–12) by in turn crushing many peoples (4:13) and the desire to live at peace. The triumph for Micah comes in chapter five in his hope for the ruler of Israel who will come out of that small town, Bethlehem: a ruler will appear and be their shepherd "in the strength of the Lord" (5:4). Micah expressed the conviction that "he shall be great to the ends of the earth; and this shall be peace" (5:4).

For the Hebrews, Yahweh was sovereign. The Lord had chosen them to be his people. They believed firmly that Yahweh's will was for peace and that eventually that peace would be established *on* the earth by God's people led by his own anointed. As Gerhard von Rad has observed, there is not one instance in the Old Testament in which *shalom* designates a specific inner attitude or internal peace. *Shalom* has to do with the many.[27] It is a social concept. It is God's gift to his people, but like all of his gifts, *shalom* needs to be appropriated and the conditions for doing so are clear. It is always possible to reject it.

NOTES

1. The word "ethics" does not really apply in either Judaism or Christianity since what is affirmed is a relationship of people to each other based on the commands of God. In the Bible there is no systematic presentation of prescribed human conduct. Rather one could speak with R. T. Herford of Jewish ethics as "teaching directed to the right conduct of life as man's service of God" (cited by A. Nissen, *Gott und der Nächste im antiken Judentum*, WUNT 15 [Tübingen: J. C. B. Mohr, 1974], 6).

2. A. von Harnack, *Marcion* (Leipzig: J. C. Hinrichs, 1921), 248–49. "To discard the Old Testament in the second century was a mistake which the great church rightly rejected; to retain it in the sixteenth century was a fate which the Reformation could not avoid; but still to conserve it as canonical is the consequence of a religious and ecclesiastical malady (Lähmung)."

3. W. Klassen, "Love Your Enemy," in *Biblical Realism Confronts the Nation*, ed. P. Peachey (Nyack, N.Y.: Fellowship Press, 1963), 153–54.

4. This section follows in the main Klaus Koch, ed., *Um das Prinzip der Vergeltung in Religion und Recht des Alten Testaments* (Darmstadt: Wissenschaftliche Buchgesellschaft, 1972) and George Mendenhall, *The Tenth Generation* (Baltimore: Johns Hopkins Univ. Press, 1973), 69–104.

5. J. Horovitz, "Auge um Auge, Zahn um Zahn," in *Judaica: Herman Cohen Festschrift* (Berlin: Bruno Cassirer, 1912), 609–58. See also Nissen, *Gott und der Nächste*, 266–67. He cites Lev. 19:18; Prov. 24:29, cf. 20:22.

6. Mendenhall, *The Tenth Generation*, 74.

7. Ibid., 75.

8. Compare G. von Rad, *Das erste Buch Mose: Genesis* (Göttingen: Vandenhoeck & Ruprecht, 1967), 90–91; A. Alt, *Essays on Old Testament History*, ET: R. A. Wilson (Garden City, N.Y.: Doubleday & Co., 1968), 136, 141; and for analogies from antiquity, A. Dihle, *Die Goldene Regel*, 20–40.

9. U. Cassuto, *A Commentary on the Book of Genesis* (Jerusalem: Magnes Press, 1961), 242–44.

10. E. I. Lowenthal, *The Joseph Narrative in Genesis* (New York: Ktav, 1973), 156, notes that in chap. 42 the principle of retaliation, measure for measure, is assumed. It is a divine principle according to *b. Sanhedrin* 90a (see also L. Ginzberg, *Legends* VII). On the other hand S. Schechter (*Some Aspects of Rabbinic Theology* [New York: Schocken Books, 1961], 204) cites numerous texts in which it is stated that humans dare not imitate God in taking revenge.

11. Plutarch, *Moralia: How to Profit by One's Enemies.*

12. Mendenhall, *The Tenth Generation,* 70. Although phrased differently, this is the theme which holds together the important essays edited by Koch, *Prinzip der Vergeltung.* Koch and Mendenhall came to similar conclusions but neither shows awareness of the other's work.

13. Mendenhall, *The Tenth Generation,* 71.

14. Ibid., 78.

15. Ibid., 83.

16. Mendenhall (ibid., 84) sees Josh. 10:12–13 as an example of defensive vindication of the group. Thus it could be translated: "until a nation had been delivered from its enemies" (v. 13) (ibid., 84–85). He states that the grammatical construction of the account in 1 Sam. 24:8–15 has been shown to have the characteristics of the Amarna letters, thus suggesting that it rests upon very old tradition. This along with a study of the words *NQM* and *SPT* (Judges 24:12) used here for the actions of God indicate that this is an appeal to the executive defensive vindication of Yahweh. It clearly sees self-help ruled out for David for "Such actions in self-help constitute a claim to an *imperium* on the part of the individual which is incompatible with and actually rebellious against the *Imperium* of Yahweh" (ibid.).

17. H. W. Hertzberg, *I and II Samuel* (London: SCM Press, 1964), 196–97.

18. Hans Joachim Stoebe, *Das erste Buch Samuelis,* KHCAT 8/1 (Gütersloh: Gerd Mohn, 1973), 430–40. The materials are treated in detail by Klaus Koch, *The Growth of the Biblical Tradition* (New York: Charles Scribner's Sons, 1969), 88, 217–20.

19. It thus became common to praise David for his kindness to all, "whether murderer, or murdered, persecutor or persecuted. I show him kindness as if he were a righteous man" (*Eccles. R.* VII.1.4, on VII.1, see C. G. Montefiore and H. Loewe, *A Rabbinic Anthology* [New York: Meridian Books, 1960], 433).

20. W. G. Lambert, *Babylonian Wisdom Literature* (Oxford: At the Clarendon Press, 1960), 101, lines 36–48; 103, lines 61–65.

21. James B. Pritchard, *Ancient Near Eastern Texts,* 3rd. ed. (Princeton, N.J.: Princeton Univ. Press, 1969), 422A.

22. Ibid., 426B.

23. S. Morenz, "Feurige Kohlen auf dem Haupt," *TLZ* 78 (1953): 187–92. See W. Klassen, "Coals of Fire: Symbol of Repentance or Revenge?" *NTS* 9 (1963): 337–50.

24. Koch, *Prinzip der Vergeltung,* 134–35.

25. Ralph Sockman, s.v. "2 Kings 6:22–23," *The Interpreter's Bible, III.* On the Elijah-Elisha narratives see Max Miller, "The Elisha Cycle and the Accounts of the Omride Wars," *JBL* 85 (1966): 441–54 who sees a circle of northern prophets at work who looked to Elisha as their ideal. "These accounts were revised by them to enhance the prophetic role in Israel's military successes and were transmitted thereafter in association with the Elisha cycle (446). Neither O. H. Steck, *Überlieferung und Zeitgeschichte in den Elia-erzählungen* (Neukirchen-Vluyn: Neukirchen, 1968) nor Leah Bronner, *The Stories of Elijah and Elisha as Polemics against Baal Worship* (Leiden: E. J. Brill, 1968) deal with our topic at any length. Hans-Jürgen Hermisson, *Studien zur Israelitischen Spruchweisheit,* WMANT 28 (Neukirchen-Vluyn: Neukirchen, 1968) explores some of the relationships between wisdom and the prophet Amos. On the theme of feeding the enemy, see above p. 19. The theme that one should eat only with good men occurs often. Musonius Rufus appeals to Theognis when he urges people to live with their teachers out in the country: "Drink and eat and sit down with good men, and win the approval of those whose influence and power is great" (XI). The assumption is that when you mingle with good men you will learn good, "but if you mingle with the bad you will destroy even such soul as you had" (ibid.; he is citing *Elegies* 33–36). The potlatch among some native Americans also obviously used eating with the enemy as a guarantee to peace. See Abraham Rosman and Paula G. Rubel, *Feasting with Mine Enemy: Rank and Exchange among Northwest Coast Societies* (New York: Columbia Univ. Press, 1971), 181, 185, 206.

26. See the important study by G. Schmitt, *Du sollst keinen Frieden schliessen mit den Bewohnern des Landes: Die Weisungen gegen die Kanaanäer in Israelsgeschichte und Geschichtsschreibung,* BWANT 91 (Stuttgart: Kohlhammer, 1970).

27. G. von Rad, "eirēnē," *TDNT* 2 (1964): 405–6.

CHAPTER 3

Judaism and the
Quest for Peace

John Piper, the author of the only book known to me in English on love for the enemy, states:

> The perceptive Jew must have viewed Jesus' love command as an attack on the Torah, first because it contradicted his understanding of Lev. 19:18, and second, because it seemed in general to devaluate the distinction between Jew and Gentile—a distinction grounded in the Torah. Jesus' command to love the enemy as well as the friend contained the seed for the dissolution of the Jewish distinctive.[1]

Since similar assertions are made by other scholars as well, and since this is one of the most fallacious conclusions current among New Testament scholars, it deserves some attention.[2] It is clear that Piper is saying that Jesus attacked the Torah—a conclusion which has not found wide acceptance. Why should a contradiction of the "perceptive Jew's" understanding of the love commandment be seen as an attack against Torah? Surely first-century Judaism was anything but a monolith. Could not Jesus' understanding of the love commandment be seen as part of the richness of first-century Judaism?

Our analysis of the sources makes it clear that the love commandment as Jesus understood it was in fact widely held in Judaism and that understanding was firmly rooted in the Hebrew scriptures. Jesus' teaching to love the enemy contained the seed, not for the dissolution of the Jewish distinctive, but for its survival after the year 70 C.E.

A view of God similar to the one we saw in Jonah, fundamental to Judaism, is found in the story of Abraham interceding for Sodom and Gomorrah. Abraham pushes his bargaining to the limit. He is not trying to save the lives only of the just. He is concerned that if at

43

least ten just people can be found that the whole city may be spared. Their presence provides hope that the just will save the city (Gen. 18:16–33).

This image of God as the God of love who searches out a people and calls them purely by reason of his love is integral to the Hebrew view of God. Israel itself was formed through an act of God's boundless love. Many Hebrew thinkers were critical of their people because they were unfaithful to God's initiative. Israel's unfaithfulness made it impossible for the other nations to be drawn by God's love. The particular interest God has in the Jews is never to be seen as an exclusive one but rather as aiming at an inclusion of all people (Isa. 60:3).

Isaiah portrays a vision of Damascus and Egypt brought together by God. These two classical enemies feared by Israel are also under the Lordship of God who will strike Egypt, "healing as he strikes" (Isa. 19:21–22). The time will come when Israel will rank with Egypt and Assyria, and the three "will be a blessing in the centre of the world" (19:24). The two countries were locked in a struggle for world domination. Israel was tempted to take sides but both were at times their enemies. The prophet Isaiah promises: "Blessed be Egypt my people, and Assyria the work of my hands, and Israel my heritage" (Isa. 19:25). Did Jesus perhaps have some such position in mind when he taught love for one's enemies? Clearly there were instances in Hebrew history to which he could appeal, as well as a theology of the manner of God's working in history.

To be sure, God's love has a jealous side, and there are times when he does not spare. Even when this happens we are dealing here not with vengeance as often understood but rather with an assertion of God's *imperium*—God's sovereignty.[3] Jeremiah threatens the unfaithful of Judah that God will destroy them all—kings, priests, and prophets—and show them no pity (13:12–14). They will be handed over to King Nebuchadrezzar, to their enemies, and they will be destroyed and God will show no pity, no mercy, and no compassion (Jer. 21:7). Ezekiel reiterates that God will show no pity to his own people (5:11; 7:4, 9). Yet one of the earliest prophets, Hosea, while he too wrestles with the vengeance and wrath of God, finally declares that God will not be like man (11:9). He will show pity to his people. In the end the two sides of God's nature are kept in tension with each other, and mercy triumphs over justice in his dealings with his people and the nations.

Closely related to this strain is the motif that God counts on his own people to assist him in rooting out the evildoer both from within the people and the outsider as well. Sodom and Gomorrah were after all destroyed—but that was done by a direct act of God. The most striking instance of this tradition appears in the Phinehas story recorded in Num. 25:1–15. The Israelites had turned their backs on Yahweh and Moses was ordered to put to death the leaders of the people. To the judges fell the grisly task of killing all those who had been unfaithful. As this was being done in order to "turn aside the fury of God's anger" (v. 4, NEB) Zimri, a chief in the Simeonite tribe, brought in Cozbi, a Midianite woman, and fornicated with her in his tent. Phinehas, filled with righteous zeal, pursued them into the tent, and with his spear killed both of them during their act of intercourse. For this deed he was rewarded with these words (Num. 25:10–14, NEB):

> Phinehas . . . has turned my wrath away from the Israelites; he displayed among them the same jealous anger that moved me, and therefore in my jealousy I did not exterminate the Israelites. Tell him that I hereby grant him my covenant of security of tenure [RSV, peace]. He and his descendants after him shall enjoy the priesthood under a covenant for all time, because he showed his zeal for his God and made expiation for the Israelites.[4]

Phinehas became the ideological founder of the zealot party. He is frequently mentioned in Jewish sources. As the priest in charge of the holy vessels during a military campaign (Num. 31:6), he gave signal for the battle-cry. Psalm 106:30–31 (NEB) praises him as one who interceded: ". . . and the plague was stopped. This was counted to him as righteousness throughout all generations for ever."

Another writer lists Phinehas as "the third in glory, for he was zealous in the fear of the Lord, and stood fast . . . in the ready goodness of his soul, and made atonement for Israel" (Sir. 45:23). The chronicler refers to him as a gatekeeper superintendent (1 Chron. 9:20) and adds that "the Lord was with him!" Joshua 22:13–29 describes him as a leader of a mission into the land of Gilead to remonstrate against the Reubenites, Gadites, and the half tribe of Manasseh for the altar they had built. But the people proved their fidelity to God, and Phinehas and his colleagues accepted the argument that if they had been unfaithful God would have punished them.

Closer to the time of Jesus, 1 Maccabees depicts Phinehas as the model for the action of Mattathias who initiated the Maccabean War, for the latter showed "his fervent zeal for the law, just as Phinehas had done by killing Zimri" (1 Macc. 2:26). On his death-bed Mattathias admonished his sons to be zealous for the law and listed Phinehas, our father, as third after Abraham and Joseph as men who were "deeply zealous" (1 Macc. 2:54).

Clearly what we have here is a different model. God's honor must be protected, and it is protected by a man like Phinehas who does not hesitate to intervene by killing one of his own people who had compromised his service to Yahweh.

In Jewish tradition current at the time of Jesus, there can be no doubt that Phinehas was one of the models of faithful and courageous service to Yahweh that was available to Jesus.

If, as Elias Bickermann has argued, the Maccabean War was as much a civil war between Jewish factions as it was against an external foe, one can readily see why Phinehas would emerge as a model to follow.[5] It has been abundantly illustrated that he was a type of the messiah who was to come who also would begin by purging Judaism of unfaithfulness, and in that bring peace because a faithful people cannot be defeated by a pagan foe.[6]

The support for such drastic action is found in the Deuteronomic Code (13:6–9). It specifies that if a member of the family entices you to idolatry, your hand is to be the first to cast a stone against him: "Nor shall your eye pity him, nor shall you spare him, nor shall you conceal him; but you shall kill him; your hand shall be first against him to put him to death" (13:9–10). Moses himself ordered that the Levites were to arm themselves with a sword and "go to and fro from gate to gate throughout the camp, and slay every man his brother, . . . his companion, . . . his neighbor" (Exod. 32:27). Having done so Moses commended them (32:29):

> Today you have ordained yourselves for the service of the Lord, each one at the cost of his son and his brother, that he may bestow a blessing upon you this day.

Clearly we are in the presence here of a model of retaining the *shalom,* the wholeness of the people, against all threats. Drastic action is required to maintain the purity of devotion to Yahweh, and in this case it is not Yahweh who intervenes but the servant of Yahweh who is energized by the same zeal which God displayed. There can be no doubt that this strain is present in Judaism and that it fed the Zealot movement of the first century. It is seen in such literary sources as the *Testament of Asher* (chap. 4) which tries to show that although an action (e.g., murder) may look evil, "the whole is good" (cf. Josephus's comment on the Zealots, *Jewish War* 7.270). It is present in the Qumran sources where hatred is displayed towards the outsider and even more forcefully against the sons of Beliar, who are members of their group but have become apostate. While we have no evidence that they were murdered, the strictness of the Essene ban was such that the sons of Beliar virtually starved to death, and it is clear that vengeance played an important part in the eschatological war. In the years 70–74 C.E. the Essenes suffered a cruel demise along with the Zealots.

The tragic event at Masada in the spring of 74 was the last fateful act of atonement. Rather than allow the Romans to sacrifice Zealots, Eleazar was able to persuade his men to kill their families, for it was now clear that they had sinned against God in beginning the war against Rome. Better that they "pay the penalty for those crimes . . . to God through the act of our own hands" than to let the Romans do so (*Jewish War* 7.333).

In addition to this tradition of Phinehas, there are several others: the tradition of Yahweh as warrior, the imprecatory Psalms in which the composers actually pray for the destruction of their enemies (Ps. 149:6–9), and the traditions of the militant messiah. These latter traditions have overshadowed the nonviolent and other traditions in Judaism which build their hopes for peace on God's own intervention but allow the followers of Yahweh no personal vengeance or even the use of weapons to kill their enemies. Is it possible to reconcile these opposite positions?

We believe it is possible. In fact, when careful research is done we will find that the dominant position which emerges—which Jesus himself espoused—was to place one's faith firmly in the sovereignty of Yahweh and at all times to respect the fact that he is Lord of life and death. We do not follow scholars like Hans Windisch who argue that the examples of nonviolent resistance found in Jewish history "show that a warlike power lies latent in this people which can be released in a given provocation."[7] Rather, we take Jewish history as a part of human history and respect the fact that even under the extraordinary provocation to which they have been brutally exposed throughout history, the Jews responded with a profound doctrine of suffering which can transform our approach to violence in history. It will not be possible to trace all of the evidence to support our position.[8] Our sources are too rich and too complex for that. We shall try to demonstrate, however, that in all sources—historical, ethical, and the prophetic—a strong position arises which binds together the themes of love towards the enemy and the pursuit of peace. When justice is done towards the oppressed or the enemy, *shalom*—peace in its profoundest and most universal sense—will reign. That is the will of Yahweh, and the path towards that peace is charted by a great prophet of Judaism, Jesus himself.

The Jewish ethic is primarily concerned with the way in which people live together under the covenant. The Jews' common life, in which they sought to keep the covenant of God and remain faithful to God's will, is one which made its imprint upon all of the Mediterranean area. During the first century in particular, Judaism was in great turmoil. There were sharp disagreements between the Essenes, who sought withdrawal from Jerusalem and public life to the caves by the Dead Sea, and the Sadducees and Pharisees, who tried to remain faithful to the God of Israel even as they lived within a pagan state. The one group made compromises and tried to save as much of the core of their faith and liturgy as possible. The other group staunchly refused any compromise and felt that God was calling them into the wilderness, there to create a new community in which justice would be established and which might prepare the way for the coming of the Messiah. There were also the Zealots who remained in the mainstream of society, brooking no compromise. In spite of what some recent writers have maintained, Jesus had very little in common with these violent revolutionaries.

While the goal of Greek ethical thought was self-knowledge, and for many happiness was the ultimate end *(telos)* of life, Jewish ethical thought revolved around the question of loving humankind, one's neighbor in particular. The fellow member of the community was the neighbor, whom we are called upon by God to love, for the neighbor is you, yourself (Lev. 19:18). While Judaism did not make happiness a goal, it assumed that one achieves happiness or blessedness by serving God out of love for him and secondarily out of fear or respect, but above all by serving one's fellow human with the same love. If we speak of happiness the Jew of the first century might argue that you become happy as you make others happy, in that you give your fellow humans evidences of goodness, help them, or lighten the burden of their lives. There is thus lacking totally in Judaism (and later in Christianity) any dichotomy between a *personal* ethic and a *social* ethic—its ethic is social through and through.

In the social organism everyone has a place, for the person is no solitary unit isolated from all others. A place must be found to allow a person's gifts and talents to develop. For this to happen, justice and love must be allowed to grow and develop within the community. Justice is the trait which prevents someone from intervening in the affairs of another, whereas love begins with the desire to further the life of the other and expresses itself in all the concrete ways possible.

> This intimate union of love with justice protected Judaism's concept of justice from becoming the highest injustice, from becoming an arid principle, a lifeless formality. Conversely an enduring contact with justice protected the Jewish idea of love from losing itself in a tidal wave of emotions and from refusing to recognize the conditions of life.[9]

Vengeance clearly is not permitted in Jewish law. To store up animosity, eventually to repay something one has suffered, or to repay evil with evil, is for Judaism not only a sin against the opponent, but more fundamentally a sin against human nature and honor.

> This is the heart of the Jewish command to love your enemy: even the enemy is and remains a person, no matter how gravely he has denied his humanity. If he has need, you must be able to forget and not deny him aid. Under no conditions may you allow yourself to be misled and follow his example, lowering yourself to his standards. To be able to forget for the sake of the man or humanity, to practice forgiveness and reconciliation, is according to Jewish teaching the highest, noblest, and most effective means to secure the existence of the whole community.[10]

The sources recognize the breadth of the love commandment. No limits are imposed on the definition of "enemy." The enemy can refer to anyone, even a non-Israelite.

The main spokesmen for Judaism and all major parties have, even when they have called for violent hatred against the enemies of God, affirmed the Gentile as a creation of God. The Passover ceremony clearly expresses this when it does not allow for the completion of the recitation of the Hallel, for according to the *Talmud* God does not rejoice in the downfall of the evil ones. When the Egyptians drowned as they were pursuing the Israelites into the sea, an angel wanted to strike up a song of rejoicing. God demurred, saying, "My creations are drowned in the sea and you want to strike up a song of praise about that?"[11] And when the hour comes when Israel's enemies will fall in the messianic age, in order to make room for the triumph of Israel the following lament sounds forth from heaven: "These and those are my creations, shall I destroy one for the sake of the other?"[12] Other sources indicate that "God himself, at the time when he is angry, has compassion on those who revolt against him and their cattle."[13]

The commandments of Deuteronomy 23 specify that the Ammonite or Moabite are never to enter the Assembly of the Lord, even to the tenth generation, "because they did not meet you with bread and with water . . . when you came up from Egypt." The Edomite and Egyptian are not to be abhorred, the former because he is a brother and the latter "because you were a sojourner in his land" (Deut. 23:3–8).

In dealing with this Philo draws some interesting conclusions:

> Mere fairness itself demands thus much (to allow them to live in your land when they have no other place to go), but he goes beyond its limits, when he considers that no malice should be borne to those whose hospitality to strangers is followed by maltreatment, for nominally they are humane though their actions are not.[14]

Both Josephus and Philo speak with pride of the humane ways in which the Jews treated their enemies even in times of war and how the lawgiver inculcated the duty of sharing even in warfare.[15]

More clearly than the Stoics, however, Philo voices the conviction that goodness done to the enemy will bring enmity to a conclusion. He believed in the power of acts of good will to dissolve enmities and saw this as the intention of the Deuteronomic law. After admiring the Deuteronomic regulations on kindness to an enemy's beast of burden,

Philo expressed the belief that when the regulation is followed and the animal is returned,

> as surely as the shadow follows the body, a termination of the feud will follow. He, the receiver of a benefit which he has not willed, is drawn towards amity by the kindness which holds him in bondage *(agetai pros to enspondon chariti doulōtheis)*. You, his helper, with a good action to assist your counsels, are predisposed to thoughts of reconciliation. This is what our most holy prophet through all his regulations especially desires to create, unanimity, neighborliness, fellowship, reciprocity of feeling. . . .[16]

Rabbi Meir, according to the *Talmud,* was often harassed by evil men on his way to the place of instruction. Tired of such treatment, he returned one day uncharacteristically full of anger and in an excited manner began to pray to God that he would soon do away with those scoundrels so that he might have peace. As he did so, his wife Beruria entered the room, heard his prayer, and sternly rebuked her husband. "Your prayer violates the holy teaching, which calls only for the destruction of sins and not of the sinners, therefore you should be praying for the improvement of the sinners but not for their death."[17] For most the teaching of Sir. 10:6 was considered valid, "Do not nurse a grievance against your neighbour for every offense" (NEB).

The oppressions of the enemy are to be endured patiently and to be seen as testings sent by God. The patient endurance of such tribulations may bring about our own salvation. The Lord will bring deliverance in good time, but in the meantime, according to Lam. 3:26–33 (NEB),

> It is good to wait in patience and sigh. . . .
> Let him lay his face in the dust,
>   and there may yet be hope.
> Let him turn his cheek to the smiter
>   and endure full measure of abuse;
> for the Lord will not cast off
>   his servants for ever.
> He may punish cruelly, yet he will have compassion
>   in the fullness of his love;
> he does not willingly afflict
>   or punish any mortal man.

This voluntary submission to suffering, through which God will eventually perform his will, is also reflected in Isa. 50:6–8 (NEB). The prophet has heard from God, and he did not disobey or turn back in defiance:

> I offered my back to the lash,
>   and let my beard be plucked from my chin,
> I did not hide my face from spitting and insult;
>   but the Lord God stands by to help me;
>   therefore no insult can wound me.

He stands secure in the knowledge that God is with him and will clear his name.

Consistent with these attitudes, later thinkers also pronounced, "Happy is he who hears abuse of himself and ignores it, for a hundred evils pass him by"[18] or "if your neighbor calls you an ass, put a saddle on your back."[19]

Judaism took pride in seeing itself not only as the carrier of but also as the sufferer for the divine teaching in which eternal values were reflected and which the nations themselves would eventually recognize.

It is better to belong to the oppressed than to the oppressors. In the countless families of birds, none is more innocently oppressed and pursued by the stronger birds than is the dove, "and it is precisely this bird which God has designated as his most acceptable offering."[20]

The Book of 2 Esdras (cf. 5:26, NEB) wrestles with the problem while affirming God's election of his people: "From all the birds that were created you have named one dove, and from all the animals that were fashioned you have taken one sheep."

Such suffering is embraced with joy:

> Belong to the persecuted and not to the persecuting, listen to insults and do not answer them, do everything out of love for God and keep a joyous courage and confidence as you suffer.[21]

Like Socrates and some of the Greek traditions seen in this study, Judaism shares the lofty conception that those who are persecuted are morally superior to their persecutors who lack compassion; that in fact the one injured has compassion on the one injuring him and that the one whose liberty is severely constrained feels himself freer than his captor.

The joining of the issue is perhaps most complete in those circles represented by the *Assumption of Moses, Joseph and Asenath,* and the *Testaments of the Twelve Patriarchs.*

THE ASSUMPTION OF MOSES

This work is dated between the years 7–30 C.E.[22] Its provenience is generally agreed to be Palestine, and the author has been variously sought "among the Zealots" or termed a "Pharisaic Quietist."[23] "He was a Pharisee of a fast-disappearing type, recalling in all respects the Chasid of the early Maccabean times and upholding the old traditions of quietude and resignation."[24] Written during the life of Jesus, *The Assumption of Moses* is of particular importance to our study.

Of central importance to this author is the death of Taxo. Taxo reminds his sons that their strength is that they have not tempted God by transgressing his commandments (9:5). He admonishes them to fast for three days, enter a cave on the fourth, "and let us die rather than transgress the commands of the Lord of Lords, the God of our Fathers. For if we do this and die, our blood will be avenged before the Lord" (*As. Mos.* 9:6–7).

So the death of Taxo and his invitation to his sons to die with him is the key to our understanding of the book. The role of Moses will be that of intercessor (*As. Mos.* 12:6) not an agent of vengeance. Neither the role of Moses nor that of Joshua is seen in zealot terms. God is everywhere and at every time the sole agent of vengeance.

David M. Rhoads sees some of the nonviolent demonstrations described by Josephus as the background for this writing. During the years 7–30 C.E., he sees little evidence of revolutionary activity but does see some of passive resistance. "In this period, the author of the *Assumption of Moses* exhorted obedient death as a way to guarantee vengeance against the enemy."[25] Vengeance is seen here as brought about by the innocent suffering of those who stay true to the Law.

JOSEPH AND ASENATH

The issue of violence appears in a book which has recently received increased attention: the apocryphal *Joseph and Asenath.*[26] There is no agreement on the dating of the book, the ranges being from 100 B.C.E. to about 200 C.E. with a consensus emerging that it is pre-Christian. We consider it Jewish; no serious argument has been made that the ethics of the book are non-Jewish.

Our interest is concentrated on chapters 23–29. There Asenath is threatened by the Pharaoh's first-born son who saw Asenath as she returned from a visit to her father-in-law and "fell madly" (became *emmanēs*) for her. The Pharaoh's son summoned Simeon and Levi and told them that having heard of their exploits against Shechem, he knew them to be stronger men than were in all of Egypt. Therefore, the Pharaoh's son asked Simeon and Levi to enter into a pact with him. He would give them much gold, silver, maids, and servants if they would fight on his side against Joseph. If they would help him to kill Joseph they would be his friends (23:4). If not, he would kill them with his sword which he drew to demonstrate its glory.

Upon seeing the sword, Simeon became very angry; but even as he thought about drawing his own sword, Levi's prophetic powers made him realize what Simeon was about to do, and he intervened giving him to understand why he should cease from his wrath (23:1–9): "Why are you moved in anger against him? For we are children of godfearing men and it is not proper for a godfearing man to repay evil for evil to his neighbor."

And Levi, in gentleness of heart and cheerfulness of countenance, said to the son of Pharaoh (23:9–10):

> Why does my lord speak of such matters to us? We are godfearing men and our father is a servant *(doulos)* of the highest God and Joseph our brother is beloved of God. [Certain manuscripts then go on:] How would it be possible for us to do this evil before God? . . . take care not to speak again such things concerning our brother Joseph. It is not fitting for the godfearing man to harm anyone who desires to harm him.The godfearing man will not defend[27] himself, for he has no sword in his hand.[28]

This is surely an unusual description of the godfearing man and how he deals with conflict. He is shown as being utterly defenseless in the face of the aggressor.

The son of Pharaoh seeks others, however, who will help him realize his plan. So the sons of Billah and Zilpah are brought, and to them he says (24:6–7):

> Behold, blessing or cursing lie before you; better choose blessing than death; you are courageous men and do not die like women; therefore be courageous and avenge[29] your enemies.

The son of Pharaoh then goes on to tell them that he has heard

Joseph say, that as soon as Jacob is dead he will get rid of his brothers and avenge their act of selling him into slavery. Dan and Gad accept his propositions and they plan to do away with Joseph and also Pharaoh during the night. The attempt to destroy Pharaoh fails. The younger brothers, Naphtali and Asher, try to dissuade Dan and Gad from their course of action, for they say that Joseph will call upon the highest who will protect him with fire from heaven, and then they will need to fight against God's angels. But the older brothers turn aside their reservations: "Do you think we want to die like women? Heavens no!" (25:8) and in their anger they proceed to execute their plan.

As Asenath sets out on her journey, Joseph bids her farewell with the assurance that Levi is with her and will protect her. She has not gone far, however, when she and her party are ambushed and many of her bodyguards are killed before Levi has a vision of what is happening and dispatches himself with soldiers to the scene.

In the meantime, Benjamin, only nineteen and beautiful in appearance, strong as a young lion and one who fears God, jumps from the chariot. Taking a stone from the brook, he throws it at Pharaoh's son, wounding him severely (27:2). With fifty stones provided by Asenath's chariot driver, Benjamin slays another fifty soldiers. When Reuben, Simeon, Levi, Judah, Issachar, and Zebulon arrive, they kill 2,706 more of the enemy (27:6).

The sons of Billah and Zilpah realize they must flee, but first they attempt to kill both Asenath and Benjamin. With drawn and bloody swords, they approach Asenath. Trembling with fear, Asenath cries for help to God, who does not allow her conversion to the true God to be rewarded by a violent death. The murderous swords of the sons of Billah and Zilpah fall from their hands and change into dust.

This miracle convinces the sons of Billah and Zilpah that God is fighting against them, and now they plead for mercy to Asenath (28:3–4).

> Protect us from our brother's hand that they may not take vengeance on us and turn their swords against us. And Asenath said to them: take courage and do not fear, for your brothers are godfearing men and they do not repay evil for evil to any man.

She then asks to go into the woods until the anger of the other brothers has cooled. In the meantime, "let the Lord judge between you and me" (28:6; cf. 1 Sam.24:14).

When the brothers arrive they desire to annihilate the guilty parties but Asenath says (28:11):

> I pray you, spare your brothers and do not evil towards them for the Lord has protected me from them for he broke their hands as wax before the fire. It is enough that the Lord Himself fought for us against them.[30]

When the son of Pharaoh revives and sits up spitting blood, Benjamin runs to him, unsheaths his opponent's sword (for Benjamin himself carried none) and prepares to slay him. But Levi grasped his hand and said:

> Under no conditions, brother, may you do this.
> We are after all godfearing men and it does not behoove godfearing men to repay evil for evil nor to trample on the fallen, nor to oppress the enemy unto death.
> Therefore come and let us heal him from his wound and if he lives he shall be our friend and his father Pharaoh will be our father.

And Levi raised up the son of Pharaoh and washed the blood from his face and bound his wounds and placed him upon his horse and brought him to his father (29:1–5).

One of the first questions which arises when reading such materials is the extent to which we are dealing with Christian interpolations. There are none in these materials, for nothing is found in this story which is unique to Christian sources;[31] indeed it would be hard to find anything here which is clearly stated in the New Testament. Rather, what we have is a battle description in which many men are obviously killed through hard fighting, but the main reason for the victory is that God is on the side of Asenath. Swords melting in the hands of foes, people getting killed by stones thrown by Benjamin, are miraculous motifs common to Yahweh's wars in the Old Testament and also in Maccabean stories. Nevertheless, the story contains strains of showing love for the enemy, and the questions of vengeance and forgiveness of the enemy are nowhere more clearly faced in Jewish or Christian literature. Even in spite of the inconsistencies, this motif shines through. It is remarkable that, as in Proverbs, the motif, love your enemy, comes from an Egyptian source—in this case a woman, Asenath!

Christoph Burchard has called attention to the fact that the series of "it is not fitting" *(ou prosēkon)* sentences in *Joseph and Asenath*[32] describe an ethic for the godfearing man which is not phrased in Christian terms. On several occasions, however, it is stated that "it is not proper or fitting for the godfearing man to repay evil for evil to his neighbor"[33] (23:9) "nor to trample on those who have fallen nor to harass his enemy to death" (29:3).

Accordingly, the godfearing man does not take the initiative in harming anyone, and if someone else takes the initiative in harming him he will not defend himself for he carries no weapons for defense.[34]

As Burchard observes, in the three places where the statement not to repay evil with evil occurs in the New Testament, it is merely an introduction to a better way:[35] "Repay no one evil for evil, but take thought for what is noble in the sight of all" (Rom.12:17); and similarly, "See that none of you repays evil for evil, but always seek to do good to one another and to all (1 Thess. 5:15) and "Do not return evil for evil or reviling for reviling; but on the contrary bless" (1 Peter 3:9).

The closest parallel to this statement is to be found in the Book of Proverbs (17:13): "If a man returns evil for good, evil will not depart from his house" (but the Greek [LXX] is *kaka anti agathon*). And there is a text from Qumran (1 QS X.16–18).[36]

> I will pay to no man the reward of evil;
>   I will pursue him with goodness.
> For judgment of all the living is with God
>   and it is He who will render to man his reward.

TESTAMENTS OF THE TWELVE PATRIARCHS: PEACE THROUGH LOVE

In the *Testaments of the Twelve Patriarchs* we have a similar emphasis on loving one's fellow. The Testament of Dan urges (5:2–3):

> Speak truth each one with his neighbor.
> So shall you not fall into wrath and confusion;
> But you shall be in peace, having the God of peace.
> So shall no enemy[37] prevail over you.
> Love the Lord through all your life.
> And one another with a true heart.

The Testament of Benjamin portrays the one who fears God and loves his neighbor as invincible. "Fear the Lord and love your neighbor," (3:3–4) seems to be his slogan. "He cannot be smitten by the spirit of Beliar, being shielded by the fear of God. Nor can he be ruled over by the device of men or beasts, for he is helped by the Lord through the love which he has towards his neighbor" (3:4–5). It is as if the ultimate defense of man is undivided love for the righteous and the sinner, for the good man has no blind spot in his eye. He shows mercy to all men "even though they be sinners" (4:2). Although they may devise evil instructions against him, "by doing good he overcomes evil," being shielded by the good and loves the righteous as his own soul (4:3). If they have a good mind, then, according to T. Benj. 5:1–5,

> will both wicked men be at peace with you, and the profligate holding you in awe will turn unto good; . . . For if you do good even unclean spirits will flee from you. . . . For if anyone betrays unto death a pious man, he repents; for the pious man is merciful to his reviler, and holds his peace. And if anyone betrays a righteous man, the righteous man prays. Though for a little while he is humbled, yet not long after he appears more glorious, as was Joseph my brother.

The good inclination knows no guile or lie or fighting or reviling (6:4). The Lord dwells in the good man and "he rejoices towards all men always" (6:4). Cain is cited as an example of the opposite: "envy and hatred of brother" (7:5). Just as the sun is not corrupted by shining on dung and mire so "also the pure mind, though encompassed by the defilements of earth, rather cleanses them and is not itself defiled" (8:3). Like Paul in writing to the Corinthians (1 Cor. 7:14) this writer assumes that the good can always afford contact with evil for it will conquer it just as the sun dries up the dung and drives away its evil smell. In contrast, God convicted Esau through the Midianites "who outwitted their brethren" (10:10).[38]

The Testament of Dan starts with a discussion of anger and its dangers to human life. Unless his children keep themselves from the spirit of lying and anger, they will perish (T. Dan 2:1). He advises them to "love the Lord through all your life and one another with a true heart" (5:3) as a defense against the forces of Beliar, until the time when Israel will repent and she will become transformed into a "nation which does God's will" (6:6).

"Keep, therefore, yourselves, my children, from every evil work, and cast away wrath and all lying. And love truth and long-suffering" (6:8).

The peace of Israel will be sustained by the "angel of peace" who will do his work to keep Israel from falling into evil if they repent (T. Benj. 6:2–6).

The strongest teaching against hatred is found in the Testament of Gad. The power of hatred to blind is graphically portrayed. Hate is deaf towards the commandment concerning "the loving of one's neighbor" and sins against God (4:2). Hatred seeks every excuse to put the enemy to death working together with Satan as stated in T. Gad 4:7:

> For the spirit of hatred works together with Satan, through meanness of spirit, in all things to men's death; but the spirit of love worketh together with the law of God in long-suffering unto the salvation of men.

He urges not only the removal of hatred, but love (6:1):

> Love each one his brother, and put away hatred from your hearts, love one another in deed, and in word, and in the inclination of the soul.

He provides a concrete formula then for dealing with conflict (6:3):

> Love one another from the heart; and if a man sin against you, speak peaceably to him, and having cast forth the poison of hate in your soul hold no guile; and if he repent and confess, forgive him.

Instead of insisting upon retaliation, the one sinned against is urged to a counteroffensive with a peaceful overture without guile, and if the offender responds with repentance and confession, simple forgiveness follows. No word is said about restitution.

But what if the enemy-offender does not respond thus but rather denies it? The writer says: "Do not get into a passion with him, lest catching the poison from you he take to swearing, and so you sin doubly" (6:4). Clearly the writer leaves the initiative with the addressee. He does not give him the excuse of trying to define the "aggressor" or to ascertain who took the initiative in sinning.

If, however, he denies it and still evidences some sense of shame when being reproved, stop reproving him for he may repent later and may not again wrong you, "yea, he may also honour you, and be at peace with you" (T. Gad 6:6). The writer gives no guarantee of what may happen to their conflict or relationship. All his statements of what may happen are tentative, but they are based rather clearly on providing a direct initiative for his reader. The initiative must always remain with the good person.

He concludes with the final and worst contingency: "If he be shameless and persist in his wrongdoing, even so forgive him from the heart, and leave to God the avenging" (T. Gad 6:7). What strikes us as strange is that there is no directive here to move to the larger society (judges, church, as in Matt. 18:17), but the whole process of vindication is conferred to a higher power. Let God take care of vengeance while you continue to forgive "from the heart!" Surely this is the sublimest and profoundest approach to human conflict evident in any of the sources we have seen. As if to build a dam even higher to contain the waters of hatred and violence, he takes up the subject of envy in the succeeding chapter and urges that instead of being envious of the one who prospers more than you, that you pray for him "that he may have perfect prosperity" (7:1). "Put away, therefore, hatred from your souls, and love one another with uprightness of heart" (7:7).[39]

The Testament of Joseph develops a different theme: covering up the faults of the brothers as an act of love. After chronicling a series of events he says: "You see, what great things I endured that I should not put my brothers to shame. Do you also therefore, love one another and with long-suffering hide one another's faults" (T. Jos. 17:2). As God has exalted Joseph so he will exalt all who walk in his commandments and his blessing will be upon them forever. He then continues (18:2–3):

> And if anyone seeketh to do evil unto you, do well unto him and pray for
> him, and you shall be redeemed of the Lord from all evil.[40]

What is remarkable about this affirmation is not only the injunction to meet evil with good and to pray for the enemy, but also the promise that meeting evil with good will result in God's act of redemption from all evil. The protection of God is available in the form of his redemption for those who meet evil with good. Shalom will come as God's people are faithful and constant in love and justice.

PSEUDO-PHOCYLIDES[41]

This brief work is a bit of wisdom literature which has been extremely popular throughout certain periods of Christian history. It is generally dated about the first-century B.C. but no agreement has been achieved about its relative merits. There seems to be agreement, however, on its Jewishness and no case has been made for Christian interpolations. The importance of keeping one's hands clean appears when he urges (32–34):

> Draw not your sword for murder but for self-defense *(amynō).*
> Try not to use it legally or illegally
> For even if you kill an enemy
> Still you defile your hands.

He also urges his readers not to become angry too quickly for anger unchecked can quickly change to murder (57–58).

The poem contains repeated admonitions on how to deal with the enemy. The individual weapon possessed by man, which no other animal has, is the word.

> Practise kind words, which greatly benefit everyone. A word is to man a weapon sharper by far than iron (123–24). This is his greatest security, the best part of the divinely given wisdom, and the educated person is far stronger than the giant (128–29). With the legal code of the Old Testament this writer affirms that if the beast of your enemy falters under its load, he is to be helped up again, and the lost and escaped grazing animal is not to be restrained (140–41). Far better to win a friend than to make another enemy (142). Harmful relations with a fellowman are to be nipped in the bud, wounds are to be healed (143). Although he urges his readers to flee all strife he also says: Do not do good to the bad person, for it is the same as planting seeds in the sea (152).[42]

Taken together all the evidence points in the direction of a Jewish ethical tract much along the lines of *Joseph and Asenath* or any of the Jewish Hellenistic wisdom literature.[43]

The writer warns his reader not to imitate the evil but to leave vengeance to justice (77).[44] While it is a difficult sentence to translate, he seems to be saying that the best way to defend oneself from revenge is to avoid shameful acts and not to imitate evil, to use *dikē* as a means to prevent vengeance.

The importance of this writing should not be underestimated. One writer argues that its importance has been grossly exaggerated, and a reading of it leaves one with the impression that he merely repeats trivialities.[45] It stands out, however, as a summary of Jewish ethical teaching. The admonition not to gird on the sword (lines 32–34) as

P. W. van der Horst notes is a rather "exceptional point of view in antiquity" and we detect there "undeniably a pacifist ring."[46]

THE ESSENES

Unfortunately, space does not permit us to deal with the Essene sources in detail. The conclusion that is increasingly accepted is that the Qumran sect taught that no personal enmities against fellow members of the community could be tolerated but that the outsider must be hated. This teaching of hating the outsider, particularly the Roman, combined with their doctrine of the messianic war makes it logical to assume that when the war against Rome broke out they were susceptible to arguments that the end had come. Therefore, at least, some of them joined the Zealots in their attack against Rome, and some even held out at Masada.[47] The reactions which Josephus described are, after all, related to the final act at Masada. The Stoic disdain for enemies exemplified so well in Josephus's description of the Essenes can easily lead to the final step: you refuse the enemy even the pleasure of killing you, and you "choose a clean death" at the hands of your fellow member of the religious community rather than life in slavery under Rome or death at the hands of a pagan.[48]

It must finally be recognized that when David Flusser attributes the origin of the "love your enemies" idea in Jesus to influence from the periphery of the Essene groups, he may be quite right and that there is no contradiction in such a position.[49] Not all people who received their initial inspiration from Martin Luther King, Jr., remained committed to nonviolence. So too, both those Essenes who later joined the revolt against Rome, and Jesus who taught that one should love his enemies, may have been deeply in contact with the Essene teaching that one should pray for his enemies. Only people who take a static view of the way ideas are transmitted would deny such a possibility. It is surely preferable to assume that the Essenes too were a community open to new events and to new interpretations of the love commandment, just as everyone must admit that whatever Jesus learned from his contemporaries, he also put together in a highly original way.

JOSEPHUS

The enigmatic character of Josephus is recognized by all who read him. Since he was a defector to the Roman side, it is understandable that he has not been considered a spokesman for Judaism. As one writer in first-century Judaism, his position in regard to violence and the way that God's people are to be related to conflict deserves analysis.

The first section that deserves analysis is the speech by Agrippa when he seeks to persuade the Jewish people not to go against Rome in war. We see it as a source for Josephus's own thinking when he wrote in the 90's.

Agrippa urged his hearers to study the strength of Rome before a decision was made. They had better decide whether they wish to fight in order to have their revenge for injustice, in which case what good is it to extol liberty? "If on the other hand, it is servitude which you find intolerable, to complain of your rulers is superfluous; were they the most considerate of men, servitude would be equally disgraceful" (*Jewish War* 2.348–50). The powers that be should be conciliated by flattery and not irritated. Certainly they should not pick on minor errors, for if they do, then mistreatment will move from secrecy to openness.

Then this interesting statement in *Jewish War* 2.351:

> There is nothing to check blows like submission, and the resignation of the wronged victim puts the wrongdoer to confusion.[50]

This is a remarkable statement, and if Josephus gave any evidence of a philosophy of nonviolence one would be tempted to find here a Gandhian point of view in the first century. It is similar to Seneca's statement in his moral essay on anger (*De ira* II.xxxiv.5):

> But if anger shall be rife on both sides, if the conflict comes, he is the better man who first withdraws; the vanquished is the one who wins. If some one strikes you, step back; for by striking back you will give him both the opportunity and the excuse to repeat his blow; when you later wish to extricate yourself, it will be impossible.

Josephus seems to be moving pragmatically.

He then argues that they have decided too late to break with Rome. That decision should have been made when Pompey invaded the country at which time they should have strained every nerve. He lists then a large number of famous countries who have yielded to imperial Rome.

When compared with all the impressive countries who are under

Roman rule, they have only one thing—their religion, according to *Jewish War* 2.390:

> The only refuge, then, left to you is divine assistance. But even this is ranged on the side of the Romans, for, without God's aid, so vast an empire could never have been built up.

Finally, he says that if they do enter into battle they will undoubtedly have to break some of their own religious laws, like that of the Sabbath, and if they do so then the very things they are fighting for— their religious observances—will be violated (*Jewish War* 2.394–96):

> All who embark on war do so in reliance on the support either of God or of man; but when, in all probability, no assistance from either quarter is forthcoming, then the aggressor goes with his eyes open to certain ruin. What is there, then, to prevent you from dispatching with your own hands your children and wives and from consigning this surpassingly beautiful home of yours to the flames? By such an act of madness you would at least spare yourselves the ignominy of defeat.

At one other point Josephus records an incident in which a group of discontented Jews marched on Caesarea to protest to Pilate the introduction of the effigies of Caesar into Jerusalem. The Jews implored the Procurator to remove the effigies and to uphold the laws of their ancestors. Pilate refused, and Josephus reports that for five whole days and nights the whole group "remained motionless in that position."

The next day Pilate took his seat on the tribunal, and under the guise of listening to their request he instead gave an arranged signal to his armed soldiers to surround the Jews (*Jewish War* 2.169–74).

> Finding themselves in a ring of troops, three deep, the Jews were struck dumb at this unexpected sight. Pilate, after threatening to cut them down, if they refused to admit Caesar's images, signalled to the soldiers to draw their swords. Thereupon the Jews, as by concerted action, flung themselves in a body on the ground, extended their necks, and exclaimed that they were ready rather to die than to transgress the law. Overcome with astonishment at such intense religious zeal, Pilate gave orders for the immediate removal of the standards from Jerusalem.

It is almost as if Josephus is illustrating the point made in Agrippa's speech. For by baring their necks to Pilate's sword rather than drawing their own, the delegation was able to secure what they wanted from the Roman official. The nonviolent delegation, ready rather to die for the law than to transgress it, was able to get Pilate to change.

Every historian records those events he considers important. He also provides them with the bias which he thinks is appropriate. Did Josephus have a Stoic side to him? Or was it the events of the Jewish War which on pragmatic grounds led him to deplore war and to isolate some of the nonviolent events of Jewish history in the first century? He did not, like his contemporaries, Yohanan ben Zakkai, Hillel, and Jesus of Nazareth, renounce violence, but it is clear that he could not become a Zealot. The grounds were psychological in part, to be sure. He had fought against Rome and knew what war was. But in part his reasons were also theological. God was in control of history, and for the present he believed firmly that Rome was destined to rule, not over Palestine only, but also over the whole world. The Jews could achieve their destiny, he believed, by submitting to Roman rule.

Josephus can be termed a coward or a traitor for taking this position only if we designate Yohanan ben Zakkai, Hillel, and Jesus as such. Surely there is no evidence that the revolt against Rome was justified in 66—to say nothing of 73, or during Hadrian's time. To exalt the last stand at Masada, but to overlook the courage it took for religious Jews in the first century to reject violence, is to look at the history of that century with blinders. It is a temptation which the historian had best resist in these days when the choices are very similar indeed, but the outcome much more ominous. Perhaps we are not impertinent to raise the question whether Yohanan ben Zakkai and Josephus and Jesus of Nazareth did not precisely by their "cowardly" approach do more for the survival of Judaism than did Eleazar ben Ya'ir and his 960 martyrs. At least there are times when the words of Euripides are right, "The deed is better if it saves your life than your good name in which you die exulting" (*Hippolytus* iii.184.501–02).

A modern writer, Michel Goldberg, in his quest for what it means to be a Jew has described in moving terms how he overcame the desire to kill Klaus Barbie as an act of vengeance for what Barbie had inflicted on his people. Having stalked Barbie to his hiding place, Goldberg resisted the temptation to kill him, choosing rather to kill "the Nazi" within himself. In reviewing the book, Paul Fussell writes,

"I'm probably not the only one who will wish he had shot Barbie. His destruction would seem a more valuable way to serve the world than an author's purging his soul."[51]

Goldberg has done more than purged his soul. He has captured the essence of Judaism and allowed love to triumph over hate and thus broken the cycle of hatred and vengeance which can only lead to human destruction.

We may conclude this section by telling a story. In Jewish writings we read of a Roman who suffered shipwreck and was washed ashore naked in Palestine. He hid behind rocks and called to some Jewish pilgrims, "I am a descendant of Esau, your brother. Give me some clothes to cover my nakedness for the sea has stripped me and I have been unable to save anything." They answered, "May your whole people be stripped as well." Then the Roman lifted up his eyes and saw Rabbi Eleazar walking with them and he called, "I see that you are an old man and that you are honoured by your people and that you know the respect God's creature deserves. Please help me. . . ." Rabbi Eleazar, who wore seven garments took one off and gave it to him. He also took him into his house, gave him food and drink and 200 denarii, accompanied him for fourteen Persian miles, and showed him great respect until he had returned him to his home.[52] Although the story is more recent than the emergence of Christianity, it is clear that in this Jewish story are found virtually all the elements of Jesus' teaching on love your enemies: sharing one's clothes, hospitality in the home, food and drink, and accompanying him or going the extra mile.

There is, therefore, no conflict between the teaching of Judaism on this matter and what Jesus himself as a first-century Jew taught. This is true especially of those strands of Judaism which had been deeply affected by Stoicism and other branches of Roman and Greek thought. Such influences are today taken for granted, for we realize that Judaism was not immune to the impact of the culture around it. Jesus himself was not isolated from them. We turn therefore to an examination of the teachings of Jesus.

NOTES

1. John Piper, *'Love Your Enemies': Jesus' Love Command in the Synoptic Gospels and in the Early Christian Paranesis*. SNTSMS 38 (Cambridge and New York: Cambridge Univ. Press, 1979), 91–92; cf. 204 n. 83.

2. Andreas Nissen, *Gott und der Nächste*, 303 passim. See my essay "The Novel Element in the Love Commandment of Jesus," in *The New Way of Jesus*, ed. W. Klassen (Newton, Kans.: Faith and Life Press, 1980), 100–114; s.v. "Enemy, Treatment of an," *Jewish Encyclopedia;* M. Lazarus, *Die Ethik des Judentums*, ed. J. Winter and Aug. Wünsche (Frankfurt: Kauffmann, 1911) II: 237ff.; and J. Scheftelowitz, "Die Grundlagen einer jüdischen Ethik," Section 2 "Treating Enemies" in *Monatschrift für Geschichte und Wissenschaft des Judentums* 56 (1912): 359–78, and also 478–79. G. F. Moore, *Judaism* (Cambridge: Harvard Univ. Press, 1927) II: 195–97. The important shift that has taken place in scholarship with respect to the importance of Jewish sources is striking. Of the four major monographs on "loving the enemy" which were published in the early part of this century (Bach, Waldmann, Randlinger, Steinmüller; see Chap. 2 n. 1), not one saw fit to give any space to Judaism's teaching on this topic. For a fine popular treatment of this topic, see John Ferguson, *War and Peace in the World's Religions* (New York: Oxford Univ. Press, 1978), 78–98.

3. Mendenhall, *The Tenth Generation*, 69ff.

4. Mendenhall, *The Tenth Generation*, 103ff.

5. E. J. Bickermann, *The God of the Maccabees*, ET: H. R. Moehring (Leiden: E. J. Brill, 1979).

6. On Phinehas as messiah and his virtual equation with Elijah see A. S. van der Woude, *Die messianischen Vorstellungen der Gemeinde von Qumran* (Assen: van Gorcum, 1957), 228–29. For his place among the Zealots see M. Hengel, *Die Zeloten* (Leiden: E. J. Brill, 1961), 154–76; W. R. Farmer, "The Patriarch Phinehas" *ATR* 34 (1952): 26–30; and H. Paul Kingdon, "The Origins of the Zealots," *NTS* 19 (1973): 74–81.

7. Hans Windisch, *Der messianische Krieg und das Urchristentum* (Tübingen: J. C. B. Mohr, 1909), 7. Compare also for similar statements Hermann Gunkel, *Israelitisches Heldentum und Kriegsfrömmigkeit im alten Testament* (Göttingen: Vandenhoeck & Rupprecht, 1916), 2, 3, 23, 25.

8. It is therefore quite in place when the volume *Non-Violence—Central to Christian Spirituality*, ed. J. T. Culliton (Toronto: Edwin Mellen Press, 1982), presents an important contribution by E. J. Crowley on the Old Testament (11–33).

9. Samson Hochfeld, "Nächstenliebe," *Die Lehren des Judentums*, ed. S. Bernfeld (Berlin: Schwetschke, 1925), 46.

10. Hochfeld, "Nächstenliebe," 47–48.

11. *b.Sanhedrin* 39b; Scheftelowitz, *Die Grundlagen einer jüdischen Ethik*, 364–65.

12. *b.Sanhedrin* 98b; *b.Megillah* 10b.

13. *m. Rabba* on Exod. ix. 19; cf. Jonah 4:10.

14. Philo, *On the Virtues* 105–8. Cf. also *m.Debarim Rabba* Par. 5.

15. *Against Apion* II.211–14; Philo, *On the Virtues* 109. Both isolate the treatment of female prisoners, for special comment. They agree with halakhic prescriptions (*m.Sifre Deut.* 21.11–12; 113a) but Philo parts ways from the teachers on the reasons he gives. He sees the reason for the month

of waiting in the consideration for the woman's feelings, while the Halakah proceeds from the viewpoint that the cutting of the hair, the clipping of the nails and the drab clothes all will make the captive woman less attractive and thus deter the Israelite from pursuing this foreign love (see B. Ritter, *Philo und die Halacha: Eine vergleichende Studie unter steter Berücksichtigung des Josephus* [Leipzig: J. C. Hinrichs, 1879], 76). In fact Josephus depicts the attitude toward the outsider as much more merciful than toward the insider for whom the penalty for minor crimes is death. "For example, the mere intention of doing wrong to one's parents or of impiety against God is followed by instant death" (*Against Apion* II.217).

16. Philo, *On the Virtues* 118–20.

17. *b.Berakoth* 10a. The distinction between sins and sinners apparently goes back to Ezek. 18:23; 33:11.

18. *b.Sanhedrin* 7a.

19. *b.Baba Kamma* 92b.

20. *b.Baba Kamma* 93a; viii.7; ix.30; *b.Shabbath* 151b; 88b; *b.Berakoth* 13b.

21. *b. Schabbat* 88b; *b.Yoma* 23a; *b.Gittin* 36b; H. Strack (and P. Billerbeck), *Kommentar zum Neuen Testament aus Talmud und Midrasch* (1922), I:370. Note that the statement, "It is better to belong to the oppressed than to the oppressors," also appears in Seneca, *Epistles* XCV.51, as a rule of nature. Whoever creates suffering violates the universal law (cf. Cicero, *De officiis* II.22), while the one suffering to a certain extent brings the world into balance (see A. A. T. Ehrhardt, *Politische Metaphysik von Solon bis Augustin* [Tübingen: J. C. B. Mohr, 1959], II:12).

22. The classic position is that of R. H. Charles, ed., *The Apocrypha and Pseudepigrapha of the Old Testament in English* (Oxford: At the Clarendon Press, 1913), 2:411, hereafter referred to as *APOT.*

23. E. Schürer, *A History of the Jewish People in the Time of Jesus* (New York: Charles Scribner's Sons, 1896), III/II: 73–83, esp. 80, and J. W. Lightley, *Jewish Sects and Parties in the Time of Jesus* (London: Epworth, 1925), 349. In the third edition (1909), Schürer no longer accepted a Zealot authorship (3,300) but termed him a "religious quietist."

24. Charles, *APOT,* 411.

25. David M. Rhoads, "The Assumption of Moses and Jewish History: 4 B.C.–A.D. 48," in *Studies on the Testament of Moses,* ed. G. W. E. Nickelsburg, Jr., SBLSCS 4 (Missoula, Mont.: Scholars Press, 1973), 53–8. J. J. Collins, "Some Remaining Traditio-Historical Problems in the Testament of Moses," in *Studies on the Testament of Moses,* 38–43. Collins concludes: "I understand TM as a definitely pacifist document. Taxo and his sons deliberately seek martyrdom. There is no question of resistance, and the resolve to die is made at a point when Taxo and his sons are not yet prisoners."

26. Christoph Burchard, *Untersuchungen zu Joseph und Asenath* (Tübingen: J. C. B. Mohr, 1965); idem, "Zum Text von 'Joseph und

Asenath'" *Journal for the Study of Judaism* 1–2 (1970–72): 3–34; M. Philonenko, *Joseph et Aseneth,* Introduction texte critique, traduction et notes (Leiden: E. J. Brill, 1968). I have consulted the translation of E. W. Brooks, *Joseph and Asenath* (New York: Macmillan Co.; London: SPCK, 1918) but the translation is my own from the text of Philonenko. G. D. Kilpatrick (*ExpTim* 64 [1952–53]: 4–8) argued for a date before 30 B.C.E.

27. *Amynomai* which generally has the meaning of responding in defense but can also mean revenge.

28. The present text is taken from Burchard, *Untersuchungen zu Joseph und Asenath,* 101. It is not in Philonenko but is in Paul Riessler, ed. and tr., *Altjüdische Schrifttum ausserhalb der Bibel,* 2d ed. (Darmstadt: Wissenschaftliche Buchgesellschaft, 1966), 529 and in the Brooks translation. Serious problems are created by this text.

29. One text had "greet" *(aspasesthe).* The text we follow has *amynomai.*

30. The last three words are not in Philonenko's text; they are found in Brooks's.

31. T. Holtz, "Christliche Interpolationen in 'Joseph und Asenath'" *NTS* 14 (1967–68): 482–97 has tried to identify the interpolations but his efforts are unconvincing. He does not deal with the ethical material.

32. Burchard, *Untersuchungen zu Joseph und Asenath,* 100ff.

33. See also *Joseph and Asenath* 28:4: *"mē apodidontes kakon anti kakou tini anthrōpō"* and 28:14: "Under no circumstances repay evil to your neighbors because the Lord will avenge such pride."

34. Burchard, *Untersuchungen zu Joseph und Asenath,* 101. For textual matters see C. Burchard, "Zum Text von 'Joseph und Asenath'" (above, n. 26).

35. Burchard, *Untersuchungen zu Joseph und Asenath,* 102.

36. Eng. trans. of 1QS X.16–18 by Geza Vermes, *The Dead Sea Scrolls in English* (Baltimore: Penguin Books, 1962), 90–91. Dieter Sänger (*Antikes Judentum und die Mysterien* [Tübingen: J. C. B. Mohr, 1980]), offers a full-length study of *Joseph and Asenath* from a history of religions point of view and concludes that the parenetic-ethical formulations in the book represent a branch of hellenistic-ethical formulations in the book related to the *Testaments of the Twelve Patriarchs* which serves as a bridge between pagan popular ethics and New Testament parenesis (220–21), Howard Clark Kee, "The Social-Cultural Setting of Joseph and Aseneth" (*NTS* 29 [1983]: 394–413), appears not to be aware of Sänger's work and unfortunately confines himself to the book as a "romance." Its latter half is clearly an ethical treatise.

37. Reading (with Perles) *polemios* for *polemos* (cf. Charles, *APOT* 2:333 n. on V. 2). The text followed here is M. de Jonge's *Testamenta XII Patriarchanum* (Leiden: E. J. Brill, 1964).

38. Charles reads "loved" (*APOT* 2:359) but de Jonge reads "outwit."

39. R. H. Charles (*APOT* 2:292–93) referred to such a text as a "passage of truly epoch-making importance" and described T. Gad 6:3–7 as "the most

remarkable statement on the subject of forgiveness in all ancient literature." It is impossible and unnecessary to go into the details of the flourishing research into the *Testaments of the Twelve Patriarchs* here. No consensus is emerging but there seems to be agreement that most of the ethical material in them is common to Jewish and Christian circles. M. de Jonge, "Recent Studies on the Testaments of the Twelve Patriarchs," *SEA* 36 (1971): 77–96, gives a good description of the latest research and conclusions. H. Dixon Slingerland (*The Testaments of the Twelve Patriarchs: A Critical History of Research* [Missoula, Mont.: Scholars Press, 1977], 102, 107, 112) assumes it is a Christian document. See also H. C. Kee's new translation of and introduction to the Testaments in *The Old Testament Pseudepigrapha*, ed. J. H. Charlesworth (New York: Doubleday & Co., 1983), 775–828.

40. Compare Ahikar, *Syr. Frag.* I.20: "if your enemy meet you with evil, you meet him with good." On this see G. Nickelsburg, ed., *Studies on the Testament of Joseph* (Missoula, Mont: Scholars Press, 1975), especially the essays by W. Harrelson and by Harm Hollander on "The Ethical Character of the Patriarch Joseph," 47–104.

41. The Greek text of Pseudo-Phocylides used as a basis is that of D. Young, ed., *Theognis, Ps. Pythagoras, Ps. Phokylides* (Leipzig: Teubner, 1961). The translation is mine but I have also consulted B. S. Easton's translation in *ATR* 14 (1932): 222–28. The whole appears also in the second book of the *Sibylline Oracles*. A masterful study of the whole document, including a translation and commentary is that of P. W. van der Horst, *The Sentences of Pseudo-Phocylides* (Leiden: E. J. Brill, 1978). See also J. J. Collins's new translation of and introduction to the *Sibylline Oracles* in *The Old Testament Pseudepigrapha*, 317–472, esp. 346–48.

42. Compare the similar statement in *Theognis,* cited above, p. 42.

43. Compare the *Letter of Aristeas*. The admonition to assist the enemy's beast of burden when it falls comes from Exod. 23:4–5. The admonition not to disturb the mother in the nest (84–85) also comes from the Old Testament law (Deut. 22:6).

44. *mē mimou kakotēta dikē d'apoleipsōn amynan.* Easton's translation, "Render not evil for evil; vengeance commit to the judges," is not exact enough. Van der Horst renders it: "Do not imitate evil, but leave vengeance to justice" (*Pseudo-Phocylides,* 166).

45. See s. v. "Pseudo-Phocylides," *Encyclopedia Judaica:* "An exaggerated importance has been attached to the work."

46. Van der Horst, *Pseudo-Phocylides,* 136.

47. The discoveries of Masada seem to establish this beyond doubt. Yigael Yadin is correct when he says, "[The Essenes] refrained from participating in wars so long as those wars were not in accordance with their concept, namely, wars preordained by God. But if they reached the recognition that the great revolt was in fact the ordained war against the Romans, there would have been no reason, in terms of their own beliefs and concepts, not to take part in

it. Moreover there is in fact direct evidence in the writings of Josephus of Essene participation in the war" (*Masada* [New York: Random House, 1966], 174). The greater openness of the Qumran sect towards humanity as depicted by Philo and Josephus never led to a command to love the enemy (see H. Braun, *Radikalismus* [Tübingen: J. C. B. Mohr, 1957], II: 107).

48. Thus a current guide book on Masada describes their death as "honourable," for "they sentenced themselves to a clean death rather than live a life of ignoble slavery under the Romans" (Gaalyah Cornfeld, *This is Masada: A Guidebook* [Tel Aviv: Bronfman Publishers, 1973], 18, 23).

49. David Flusser, *Jesus* (New York: Herder & Herder, 1969), 74–76.

50. Flusser first called my attention to this passage.

51. Michel Goldberg, *Namesake* (New Haven, Conn.: Yale Univ. Press, 1982). Fussell's review is found in the *New York Times Book Review*, Sept. 5, 1982, 3, 14).

52. *Eccl. Rabba* 11, 1 (28c). See also *b. Yom tob* 32b (Rab, bAl). Cited and commented on by Nissen, *Gott und der Nächste*, 75–76.

CHAPTER 4

Jesus as
Prince of Peace

INTRODUCTION

Some have argued that the New Testament sources give us no reliable historical clues to the question: Who was Jesus of Nazareth? It is a matter of critical import. Was he a revolutionary dedicated to violence? Was he a gentle person, meek and mild, concerned only about teaching people how to submit to injustices whenever they came their way?[1]

These two extremes have both been shown of late to be untenable. The truth lies somewhere in between.

I reject both the extreme scepticism which says we can know virtually nothing about Jesus and also an extreme credulity which assumes that all of the gospel accounts are equally reliable.[2] Above all, I am convinced that each age must turn again to the early church's portrait of Jesus to test it for its authenticity and to test it by applying it to its own time and culture. The authors of the various gospels in the New Testament and the traditions that have been preserved for us outside those gospels have to be treated with discrimination. The variety that exists among the various accounts is not negligible. It provides us with evidence that the traditions about Jesus had a certain fluidity.

There is, however, a striking uniformity in all of the accounts. In none of the gospels is Jesus ever described as having advocated the death penalty for anybody as prescribed in the Old Testament (Deut. 13:9; 22:22–24; cf. John 8:1–11) or as having urged that his disciples or his people should take up arms against Rome. He never used his powers to destroy, except on the occasion of the cursing of the fig tree

(Matt. 21:18–19; Mark 11:12–14). Problematic as this latter incident may be for the ecologist and for those who worship a Stoic Jesus, the importance of human life is not at issue.

Nevertheless each gospel writer has his own particular portrait of Jesus. It is, therefore, important to look at these in the light of the evidence before us.

PEACE IN THE GOSPEL OF MARK

The Gospel of Mark, which shows the least interest in the ethical teachings of Jesus, also provides the least direct reference to Jesus as Prince of Peace. Only once does the noun peace *(eirēnē)* appear— when Jesus dismissed the hemorrhaging woman (5:34). Mark appears to be more fundamentally concerned about the significance of Jesus as the one who prepares the way and does not spend much time describing the content of the way or its implications for such matters as peace.

Nevertheless Mark lays an important foundation for our understanding of Jesus. Mark portrays Jesus as the one who inaugurates the Kingdom, a Kingdom in which service ranks higher than ruling or dominating. Jesus serves by healing those afflicted and "trembling with fear" by telling them: "Your faith has made you well; go in peace" (Mark 5:34: cf. Matt. 9:22; Luke 8:48; 7:50). It is a kingdom in which anyone who is "not against us" is considered to be on our side (9:40). Although the title, Prince of Peace, does not appear, it is clear that the suffering servant model of Jesus' servanthood is very prominent in Mark. The statement found both in Matthew and Luke "I have not come to bring peace, but a sword" (Matt. 10:34–35; cf. Luke 12:49–53) is missing in Mark. One brief saying of Jesus is found only in Mark: "Have salt in yourselves, and be at peace [verb] with one another" (9:50).

This saying, difficult to comprehend not only because of the way the text has been transmitted but also because it is not clear how the imagery of salt is used, makes one point clear. Jesus agrees with the Psalmist that to delight in life, to live a long life enjoying all good things, one must turn from evil and do good, to seek peace and pursue it (Ps. 34:14). This allusion to Psalm 34 is wholly consistent with Hebrew thought that the righteous one who walks in the way of Yahweh lives at peace with his fellow humans. This is so, not because peace has been made a priority, but because it is a natural outcome of living according to the Torah. "When the Lord is pleased with a man and his ways, he makes even his enemies live at peace with him" (Prov. 16:7, NEB). According to Jesus, his disciples have a responsibility to be at peace. Like many rabbis before and after him, Jesus placed a high premium on the pursuit of peace and saw it both as a gift of God but also as something which had to be pursued.

Fundamental to Mark's view of Jesus is the fact that he voluntarily gave his life and that his sacrifice was vindicated. Mark invites people to "the way." For him that "way" is none other than Jesus himself who lived for others, died for others, and asserted his sovereignty over nature, disease, and the demonic, thus laying the foundation for peace.[3]

MATTHEW: JESUS AS A JUST KING[4]

Matthew portrays Jesus as a king who brings justice (3:17). The narratives of his birth depict Jesus as the King who is above all other kings and threatens Herod's throne. The pagan wise men come to do obeisance to the infant Jesus.

Only Matthew's version of the teachings of Jesus provides the beatitude: "Blessed are the peacemakers, for they shall be called sons of God" (5:9). This is a striking formulation since Josephus, 1 Maccabees (6:49, 58; 11:51; 13:37; 14:11), 2 Maccabees (1:4), and other ancient sources also use the term. Peacemaker for many was the military commander who takes his army to pacify the countryside. For President Reagan, too, the term is used to describe a horrendous instrument of war!

To be a peacemaker means for Matthew that you will be rewarded with the status of sonship. It is the only beatitude which has such an exalted promise attached to it. The peacemakers will get their reward: sonship will be conferred on them.

The promise of being a child of God comes from the thought world of the Jews: If you take my words to heart (Prov. 2:1), if you study Torah and fulfill the commandments you will be a child of God. "Their souls will cleave to Me and to all My commandments, and they will fulfill My commandments, and I will be their Father and they shall be My children" (*Jub.* 1:24–25 Charles, *APOT,* 2:12). But it is, above all, the "just man" who is described as a "child of God" in the

Wisdom of Solomon (2:13, 16; 5:5). It is clear that Matthew sees Jesus along such lines, although this Christology of the suffering of the just one is also nurtured by the Greek tradition. It is found at a quite primitive stage of New Testament Christology.

Peace is highly praised in Jewish sources as well. "Blessed is he who implants peace and love" states the writer of the Parables of Enoch (*2 Enoch* 52:11), but it has been impossible to find the precise connection used here in Matthew of sonship and peacemaking.

Nevertheless, Hebrew writers such as Isaiah (45:7) describe Yahweh as one who makes peace alongside of evil and also as one who creates peace in the heavens (Job 25:2). Most important is the designation: Yahweh is Peace, which teachers derived from Judg. 6:24 as a normative definition of the nature of God. Hananiah, the last prefect of the priesthood, asserted that peace is as important as everything else God created.

A connection between being a "man of peace" and a son of God is also made in the Solomon narrative (1 Chron. 22:9–10), but it is also clear that Solomon is not called a son of God because he made peace. God is the peacemaker in this narrative, not Solomon. Jewish commentators used Aaron as a prototype of peace, not Solomon. Nevertheless this is the earliest text in which a combination between sonship of God and peacemaker is made, and it can therefore be assumed that it is the basis for the Matthean beatitude. In other texts the Messiah is viewed as someone who brings peace.

We conclude that Solomon is seen as a son of God (2 Sam. 7:14) and as a man of peace. What is missing is any explicit connection between the two as we have it in Matthew.

More important is the way in which the title peacemaker is applied to the caesars of New Testament times. Dio Cassius, in particular, described Caesar Commodus and Julius Caesar "as peacemaker of the world." Alexander the Great is described as both a peacemaker and a son of God. By making this connection Matthew has obviously equated the humble Christians, to whom he wrote, with the highest emperor of his time.[5]

In Matthew's version of the Sermon on the Mount it is clear that to be a peacemaker is to outwit the opponent using the tactic of surprise and refusing to retaliate in the way the opponent expects.[6] His illustrations for the teaching of love your enemy differ from those of Luke, as in Matt. 5:38–48:

> You have heard that it was said, "An eye for an eye and a tooth for a tooth." But I say to you, [1.] *Do not resist one who is evil.* But if any one strikes you on the right cheek, turn to him the other also; and if any one would sue you and take your coat, let him have your cloak as well; and if any one forces you to go one mile, go with him two miles. Give to him who begs from you, and do not refuse him who would borrow from you. You have heard that it was said, "You shall love your neighbor and hate your enemy." But I say to you, [2.] *Love your enemies* and pray for those who persecute you, so that you may be sons [children] of your father who is in heaven; . . .

The passage then concludes: Receive the reward of loving more profoundly than tax collectors. Salute all, not just your colleagues. Demonstrate that superior devotion which comes from being a child of God. Be mature in your love as God is mature in his. Retaliate as God retaliates. Matthew's examples tend to come more from Jewish wisdom literature and contain no new content. They differ profoundly from the illustrations provided by previous wisdom literature in that they stand under the rubric of loving the enemy and not resisting evil. The illustrations do not appear in such a context in previous literature. In Matthew's account Jesus brings them all under this rubric in a singular way.

The illustrations in Matthew's account come from interpersonal relations of conflict and insult, and do not dip as deeply into the economic sphere as they do in Luke. It is clear that Matthew's community has a concern for justice and is particularly concerned about the way in which the teaching of Jesus relates to Jewish scripture. Matthew tries to demonstrate that, although there are differences between the way Jesus teaches the way of peace and the ancient law, there is also continuity (5:17–18).

The strongest evidence for this appears in long quotes which Matthew provides repeatedly from the Old Testament sources. In Matthew 12, Jesus is described as having come to a point of confrontation with his opponents to the degree that they wish to kill him. He retreats into the wilderness, and Matthew describes this as a fulfillment of Isa. 42:1–4 in 12:18–21:

Behold, my servant whom I have chosen,
  my beloved with whom my soul is well pleased.
I will put my Spirit upon him,
  and he shall proclaim justice to the Gentiles.
He will not wrangle or cry aloud,
  nor will any one hear his voice in the streets;
he will not break a bruised reed,
  or quench a smouldering wick,
til he brings justice to victory;
  and in his name will the Gentiles hope.

Matthew tries to demonstrate, by the use of this section from Isaiah, that Jesus does not give up his pursuit for justice (the rights of the poor) by refusing to affirm his rights. But, in fact, Jesus leads justice on to triumph by becoming a suffering servant.[7] Justice plays an important role in Matthew's Gospel. By showing us the posture and stance of Jesus as a suffering servant and what he accomplished, Matthew brings two motifs together. By the way Jesus receives injustice, he becomes a king who brings justice to others.

Perhaps more important is that Matthew alone places this quotation immediately after the report that "the Pharisees went out and took counsel against him, how to destroy him" (Matt. 12:14). Both Luke and Matthew indicate that opposition to Jesus crystallized very early. In Luke this opposition even heightens to an attempt to lynch Jesus during his first appearance in the synagogue at Nazareth (Luke 4). Thus, we can safely assume that the opposition to the teaching and practice of Jesus came early (Mark 3:6).

According to Matthew, Jesus, early in his work, already absorbed the message and style of Isaiah and decided to respond to the threat of his own death along nonviolent and indeed nonconfrontational lines. By retreating from the conflict and refusing to assert his own rights or engaging in public demonstrations or affirming his essential benevolence, Jesus leads justice on to victory. In his refusal to engage his enemies, he fulfills the hopes and expectations of the Servant of Isaiah. By helping the weak and by giving up his life, he affirms justice and thus becomes a source of hope to the nations.

The false dichotomy sometimes made by moderns between peace and justice clearly does not exist for the Jewish Christians of the first century. A very important statement in this regard is James 3:18:

"True justice is the harvest reaped by peacemakers from seeds sown in a spirit of peace" (NEB). It could not be put more succinctly.

Throughout Matthew's Gospel, Jesus appears as the king. He embodies, however, a particular kind of kingship which Matthew supports by a very selective use of quotations from Old Testament scripture. Muted in Matthew's Gospel is the conflict, known from other sources, between the Samaritans and the Jews. Instead, in Matthew's world the key question seems to be, how should Christians relate to the synagogue? What did Jesus say that could help the early church come to terms with their fellow Jewish believers?

The answer is provided in a number of parables—for example, the parable of the two sons in Matt. 21:28–32. Likewise, the conclusion which Matthew's Gospel draws to that parable (unique to Matthew) indicates that those who seem to be the least likely candidates for membership in the kingdom (tax gatherers and prostitutes) are, in fact, pushing ahead to get in, while those whom one would expect to seek membership are not interested.

The most explicit answer, however, appears in Matthew 23, often cited as an instance in which Jesus did not himself practice what he preached. What is offensive about these verses is not so much what is attributed to Jesus himself, as what has been made of them in subsequent Christian history. These verses have been used to justify anti-Semitism and the hatred of Christians toward Jews. The eradication of Jews, wherever Christians had the dominant position, was made easier when Christians remained aloof and if they did not initiate or participate in the persecution. In Matthew 23 Jesus is depicted as blasting the doctors of the Law and the Pharisees as hypocrites six times, and Matthew knows that they will go where there is wailing and gnashing of teeth (24:51). They are called "snakes and vipers' brood" and Matthew does not, like Luke (23:37–39), lament the fact that they do not know what makes for peace.

THE CONTEXT IN THE LIFE OF JESUS

It is possible to take Matthew 23 as Jesus' words to the members of his own fraternity.[8] If Matthew has access here to genuine traditions about what Jesus actually said, we may view his statements as a manner of confrontation which often exists between people who are very close to each other. In terms of ordinary human intercourse, only people who love each other very deeply will speak thus to each other. Even if Jesus were not a Pharisee, he had friends among them, and many of his views reflect positions common among first-century Pharisees. The anti-Pharisaical Jesus may be a product of later Christian tradition and its conflicts with Pharisees of a later generation. Luke 13:31 provides evidence that Jesus had friends among the Pharisees. It is surely possible that Jesus was a Galilean Pharisee and that his conflict was limited to the Pharisaical hierarchy (scribes?) from Jerusalem. If so, this entire tirade, and all fragments of it, would need to be considered along the lines of the Jewish affirmation that those who love you most dearly are also those who rebuke you most severely.

A further observation may be made with respect to the form in which these statements are couched. The woe is a prophetic cry which must be sharply distinguished from the curse. The curse is a wish or a prayer and, as in all Hebrew stress on speech, carries a particular power to accomplish what it desires. It condemns a person to separation from God, destruction, ill-health, and the like. It is impossible to get out from under a curse.

Just as it is impossible to call back a blessing (compare the story of Jacob and Esau in Genesis 27), so it is impossible to influence a curse once it has been delivered.

The woe, on the other hand, is of quite a different nature. It is a solemn prediction of what will happen if you do not change your ways. It sounds the alarm that unless you change direction, this or that disaster will follow. Consequently the woe must always be seen as an act of love spoken on the part of those who care enough to express it.

To be sure, the reading of this chapter in church today, or in any other assembly, gives an impression of rudeness and insensitivity. If Jesus indeed spoke these words to an audience before him, it is extremely doubtful that in oral form they would create the same impression. For one thing, the tone of his voice, the expression on his face, and the way in which his audience would get involved in the discussion of these issues needs to be considered. What appears to us as unmitigated invective, may have been a powerful device to have his audience reflect on their covenant obligations and the consistent external behaviour, and, above all, the way in which one promotes the way of peace.

It is fundamentally important that we do not allow one series of statements to change the total perspective of Jesus as a peacemaker which we have from the rest of the gospels. For one thing, it is only Matthew who presents these statements in such a sharp form. His doing so must surely have something to do with the state of discussion between Jews and Christians at that time. No doubt Matthew is selecting and perhaps intensifying the conflicts between Jesus and his Pharisaic colleagues for his own purposes. While we could argue that they are, nonetheless, by virtue of this uniqueness, genuine with Jesus, nevertheless they are only a part of the picture. It is clear that Jesus had Pharisees among some of his best friends, that indeed on at least one occasion (Luke 13:31) they expressed their friendship toward him by warning him not to go to Jerusalem or risk losing his life, and that in many ways the ties between him and the Pharisees were much closer than the ties between him and the Sadducees, the Essenes, and certainly the Zealots. Jesus joined his Pharisaic brethren in his commitment to the way of Yahweh, and both shared a desire to take seriously the nature of their peoplehood under God.[9] Even in this it could be argued that Jesus was a genuine bringer of peace.

THE CHILD OF PEACE IN LUKE[10]

Luke is above all the one who portrays Jesus as a bringer of peace. From the very beginning in Luke 1 the aspirations of the Jewish people are expressed in the song of Mary and the song of Zechariah. In both cases the way of peace is something that is longed and hoped for, and it is clear that for Luke, if not for these Galilean peasants, Jesus will fulfill those expectations and those hopes. Whether these forms go back to Maccabean times, or even have Zealot overtones, is impossible to say with certainty. The fact, however, that John's mission is seen in terms of renewal, conversion, and reconciliation (1:16–17) while that of Jesus is defined in political terms, is worth noting. He will be given a throne and he shall be King of Israel (1:32–33).

In her song Mary (Luke 1:46–55) announces the rout of the arrogant of heart and mind, the lowering of imperial powers from their thrones, and the exaltation of the humble. The hungry will be satisfied and the rich be sent away empty (1:53). The climax comes in

Zechariah's prophecy where the deliverer's role is ascribed to Jesus who will deliver the Jews from their enemies, out of the hands of all that hate them. They will be rescued from enemy hands and they will be free from fear, able to worship God with uprightness of heart (1:69–75). Zechariah was grateful for the tender compassion of God for he saw himself as living with his people under "the shadow of death." Someone had come to guide their "feet into the way of peace" (1:78–79). We can perhaps understand the anxiety under which Zechariah lived. For us as well the "cloud of death" is real. No one can be accused of being a "nervous Nelly" (a favorite term of Lyndon B. Johnson's for peace activists) who takes that cloud seriously and seeks to do anything in his or her power to remove it.

Luke, however, does not remain in a state of anxiety about the cloud of death but affirms his faith that in the coming of Jesus a way of peace has indeed come into being.

Most strongly, this is expressed in Luke 2 in the announcement of Jesus' birth. Here the promise is made that peace will come to earth through the birth of this one announced by the angels.

The angelic chorus sings "Glory to God in highest heaven" and promises "on earth peace among men with whom he is pleased" (2:14). There is agreement among scholars that the older translations of this verse ("men [i.e., people] of good-will") deserve correction. The text refers to those who are favored by God. It is illuminating to compare a doublet Luke presented on the occasion of the entry of Jesus into Jersalem.

Luke 2:14	*Luke 19:38*
(sung by the angels):	(sung by the disciples):
Glory to God in highest heaven	Peace in heaven and
and on earth peace to people	glory in the highest.
whom his favor rests.	

Whereas the angels promise peace to the earth, the disciples (only in Luke's account), towards the end of Jesus' ministry, celebrate the fact that peace has come to heaven. Raymond Brown sees this as support for his view that the infancy canticles were "once applied to a christological moment later in the career of Jesus."[11] What Luke indicates is that the disciples recognized and publicly acknowledged what the angels declared in the theophany of Luke 2: the presence of the messianic king. What Brown does not pursue is that in Luke's version that messianic kingship expressed itself above all in the establishment of peace in heaven and on earth.[12] The messianic nature of Jesus is seen particularly in the fact that he has established peace.

For Luke's contemporaries who celebrated the Augustan peace, and who had become accustomed to hailing Augustus as the "savior of the whole world," and who celebrated his birthday as "the birthday of the God which has marked the beginning of the good news for the world" (Priene inscription), this deliberate juxtaposition of the birth of Jesus and the peace which he brought with that of Augustus must have been striking. It was Luke's way of confronting his contemporaries with the radical difference between the peace promised by the Roman emperor and that peace which Jesus the Christ had brought. The peace of Christ follows Jewish precedent in affirming that it begins with the persons on whom God's favor rests (see especially Isa. 48:22; 57:21, and *1 Enoch* 1:8).

Clearly this is an important affirmation for Luke. He has considerable investment in portraying Jesus as the peacemaker to the believers and to the whole world.

JESUS AND SAMARITAN VENGEANCE

The broader strokes of Luke's picture of Jesus as the bringer of peace to mankind come, no doubt, from Luke's urbanity and his desire to communicate the gospel beyond the reaches of the Jewish faith. For this reason also he placed so much emphasis on the Samaritans. They are portrayed as people who are open to Jesus' message of peace. Although they are tied to traditional ways of refusing hospitality for the Jews (Luke 9:51–55), Jesus himself does not retaliate against them.

Luke portrays the Samaritans consistently in a good light. Thus, of the ten men who were healed of leprosy, it is the Samaritan who comes to give thanks (17:16). But the high point clearly comes in Luke 10, in the Parable of the Good Samaritan. It is a Samaritan who overcomes his own history of terrorism and banditry who—in contrast to the Levite and the priest—becomes a neighbor to the man who fell among thieves. Samaritans placed emphasis on vengeance and on occasion terrorized the Jews (Josephus, *Jewish Antiquities* 20.6, 1–3). This Samaritan was different.

The priest and the Levite possibly did not wish to risk violating the rules of ritual cleanliness in case the man was in fact dead. The Samaritan was bound by similar rules but risked their violation. For him, to perform the act of loving his neighbor and to express love both toward God and his neighbor took precedence over ritual cleanliness.

This is one of the most striking examples in Luke of how the concept of love your enemy emerges in the parable to surprise the listeners and catch them off guard. As always, this is a point of the parable: that it offers a surprise, sometimes a comical surprise. For centuries scholars have sought ways to interpret the Parable of the Good Samaritan. Only those who have seen the parable as an illustration of the love your enemy teaching have interpreted it correctly.[13]

One other incident Luke reports shows that Jesus did not avenge an insult to him by the Samaritans. He describes how Jesus and his disciples, while on the way to Jerusalem, sent messengers ahead of them to make arrangements for lodging in a Samaritan village. When they were turned away because they were clearly intent on going to Jerusalem, James and John made a suggestion: Lord, if you wish, we will call fire down from heaven and destroy them. (Luke 9:54). Apparently the suggestion came from their attempt to emulate Elijah who dealt with his enemies in that fashion. It is also possible, of course, that Luke's account of this was affected by the events which took place between the Jews and the Samaritans just before Felix was appointed.

Samaritans had a particular interest in vengeance. Jesus rejects the idea decisively with some ancient texts adding: "you do not know what manner of spirit you are of" (Luke 9:55). He is preparing the disciples for a much more drastic and painful rejection than the one the Samaritans have just dealt them. So he indicates to the disciples that he bears the Samaritans no ill-will but simply moves on to another village.

After the discourse with Elijah and Moses (the prophets and the Law) on the Mount of Transfiguration, Jesus lives by a totally new and untried view of God. Both the spirit of Elijah and the law of Moses were being rendered obsolete by the decision of Jesus to follow the way of the cross. As George Caird has put it: He is entering a spiritual region where even Moses and Elijah can no longer bear him company. Often in the past the church's enemies have been dealt with more in the spirit of Elijah than in the spirit of Jesus. "Indeed Elijah might today be regarded as the patron saint of the international policy which relies so heavily on calling down fire from heaven."[14] Jesus rejects that policy and instead moves on to Jerusalem knowing that eventually the Samaritans will profit from his sacrifice and will find a way to overcome their deep commitment to a theology of vengeance.

LOVE YOUR ENEMIES

Most striking, however, is the central place which Luke gives to the "love your enemy" teaching in his Sermon on the Plain (Luke 6:20–49). As in Matthew it appears as a bold imperative unheard of in the ancient world. The idea was meant to counter that bit of folk morality which said "love your neighbors and hate your enemies." That aphorism is so well known as to need no documentation (see Chap. 1) and, indeed, it shows up in the Old Testament as an accusation of David at a time when he showed benevolence toward Absalom. He was treated as if he had lost his sanity because he loved those who hated him and hated those who loved him (2 Sam. 19:6).

The place of this teaching in the life of Jesus should not be overestimated, nor should it, however, be overlooked. Even the most skeptical of scholars have admitted that the "love your enemies" saying in the form of a command goes back to Jesus. Bultmann argued that it had to be genuine because it was not found in Judaism. The grounds for his acceptance of the statement as genuine need to be rejected since the idea is certainly present in Judaism, although the precise imperative form has not so far been located. If we are dealing here with a genuine word from Jesus, why has it had so little attention since the second century?[15] At that time it was the most quoted saying of Jesus. Why is it that in the English-speaking world only recently have scholars turned their attention to it?

The simple formula—four words in Greek, three in English—is such a surprising, radical inversion of common folk morality that one is tempted to suggest that Jesus spoke it with a twinkle in his eye (Luke 6:27, 35).

THE MEANING OF LOVE

A touch of humor is implicit in the statement, given the energy that humans throughout history have devoted to destroying their enemies.

It stands as an absolute command. Generally scholars agree that neither the term "love" nor the term "enemy" can be restricted in any way if we want to do justice to what Jesus said. The word love *(agapaō)* denotes, as always in the New Testament, an act of will and of self-giving. Here in Luke as well as in Matthew it is grounded in that love which God has shown and continues to show to his creatures. The model for this kind of behavior is God. The sanction for loving the enemy is simply to participate in the nature of God, to retaliate as God does,[16] or to be indiscriminating in our love (Matt. 5:45) or to participate in God's benevolent nature (Luke 6:35).

All utilitarian support for the commandment is undercut. It may indeed be that by loving your enemies you will change them into friends, but there is no hint of this in the statement. It may also be that by loving your enemies you will have no enemies, as the *Didache* (1:3) put it later, but again no hint of this is found in our text.

Instead, the early church took it as a dominical command. Jesus as Lord needs no support for the command from the Old Testament but simply speaks it by virtue of his person and his perception of the meaning of God's love for human relationships. Furthermore, this is a precise prescription of the form in which God's love intervenes when there is animosity or opposition between human beings. God is present in human conflict in the person of the one expressing a relationship to him by loving the enemy.

The clarity with which this command rings forth has disturbed the church without end. Every attempt has been made to circumscribe and attenuate the meaning of both the verb as well as the noun. Enemies, accordingly, are divided into "personal," "religious," "national" enemies, and any one or several of these categories are bracketed out. Surely Jesus could not have meant "political" or "national" enemies! It may be instructive to reflect on the fact that although the command to love enemies is always in the plural, thus presumably including *all* enemies, the command to love the neighbor is always in the singular. From a human point of view it would be much simpler if we could reverse those two and allow us a choice on the enemy whom we might find it expedient to love and love our neighbors always in the abstract plural! But the text does not give us that option.

Both Matthew and Luke give us a considerable number of concrete examples about what "love" means. It is important that we recognize them as examples or illustrations, for we get ourselves into extreme difficulty if we treat them as commandments on the same level and with the same degree of urgency as the overall commandment which stands at the centre, namely, the commandment to "love your enemies."[17] As we break these illustrations down, however, we notice that they have a particular economic and personal perspective, as for example in Luke 6:27–36 (au. trans.):

> But I say to you that hear, [1.] *Love your enemies,* do good to those who hate you, bless those who curse you, pray for those who abuse you. To the one striking you on the cheek, offer the other one and from the one who takes away your coat do not withhold your shirt. To the one who asks, give. From the one seeking to borrow, don't turn away. As you want others to treat you, treat them. (Sinners love those who love them. Sinners do good to those who treat them well. Sinners loan money expecting repayment: 6:32–34.) By contrast [Greek, *plēn*][2.] *You must love your enemies.* Do good. Lend without giving up hope. Reason: Become children of God. God is compassionate and so are his children.

These illustrations have one thing in common. They make you accessible and vulnerable to your enemy beyond what the enemy has already in fact done through his own initiative. In each case, as a follower of Jesus you take the initiative with a tactic of surprise going beyond what the enemy has done. Each one of these actions is also consistent with the nature of love. Love means to put your own priorities and desires second to the one whom you love. To love the enemy then means to live for the enemy, to share with the enemy that which you have, and rather than seeking to destroy the enemy, to do that which will enhance the good of the enemy and enrich the life of the enemy. To love the enemy means to place yourself at his service. It is not to abdicate power but to use power creatively. The one who loves the enemy in this way retains power and uses it cooperatively.[18]

On the face of it such counsel is, from a human standpoint, patent absurdity. It is perhaps this total absurdity which has made it impossible for the church to take this counsel seriously. It has always been allowed that certain minority groups of the church who have withdrawn from the "real" world should take the lead and represent this point of view to the world. "Responsible" Christians know, of course, that it will never be feasible for the majority of humankind.[19] It never occurs to us that this teaching is no more absurd than the cross itself.

It is striking that both Matthew and Luke see this as the way in which the disciple gives evidence of his relationship to God and that to do this is not any prudential guidance but rather the normal consequence of following Jesus in daily life.

Strange that already Socrates saw that to get beyond the ideal of repaying evil for evil was so radical that few people in the world would ever espouse it and even fewer would practice it. Before we dismiss this statement as a total absurdity, spoken by someone who was out of touch with reality, we should take a look at the possibility that this "unthinkable" solution to human conflict may have more wisdom in it than all the alternatives we have put in its place.

The fundamental question is the rationality of the concept of the enemy per se. Only fools live life as if they have no enemies. Equally foolish, however, is the notion that enemies lurk everywhere and that the whole world is out to get us. In between these two extremes, rational people, communities, and nations must take their stand and find a way to live with dignity and humanity.

WHO IS THE ENEMY?

The teachings of Jesus give us no guidance on how one is to determine who is an enemy and under what conditions that category has to be taken seriously. For Jesus' disciples there was no need to be explicit. Both the state and the church have been more helpful in this respect. It did not take long within the history of the church to have the Jews designated as the enemies of the church, and many demonic ways were used to cope with what was perceived as a threat from that quarter to the strength of the Christian community. For the gospel writers it was anyone who persecuted them or oppressed them.

In modern times the state has arrogated to itself the task of defining the nature of the enemy and helping us to put that label on people. Nations like Iran can change almost overnight, and perhaps the surprise of our century is the speed with which China changed from "enemy" to "friend."

These illustrations demonstrate what a farce the whole matter is. The state has no authority to prescribe for the church who is the enemy. For the church the enemy is always that which seeks to intervene between us and our accomplishment of the will of God. The state too often creates or maintains enemies because the notion still seems to prevail that it is healthy for a state to have external enemies so that its internal weaknesses may not be too apparent.

The church takes seriously the category of enemy, more seriously indeed than does the state. But it also affirms that under the cross of Christ a way has been found to overcome all enemies by drawing them into the sphere of God's love. The state can then, under certain circumstances, become the enemy to the church. The state does that when it promotes the growth of hatred, the increase of murder, the increase of the violation of human rights, and the increase of oppression. From the perspective of the church all of these are hostile acts. In every case the mandate is clear and it subsumes all others: those who follow Jesus as members of the body of Christ are commanded to love our enemies.

With respect to this command, as with respect to all that Jesus taught, the verdict applies: Christianity has not so much been tried and found wanting, as it is still wanting to be tried. Far too much ink has been wasted on the attempt to convince us of the difficulty and impossibility of carrying out this command. No useful purpose is served by describing it as something that can be done easily. What is important is to see the perspective from which this commandment must be viewed and the way in which it is reinforced by the greatest infusion of energy the world has ever seen: Jesus who not only taught but consistently lived this teaching and by so doing created a new perspective.

The test on which the teaching survives or fails is the question of whether it can be done. Once it is demonstrated that someone has loved his enemies, then it is no longer impossible. From every angle it seems clear that Jesus not only taught this concept, but lived it fully. He took his enemies seriously, he did not ignore them, but engaged them in continuing evidence of his love. " 'This man' has not been a failure yet; for nobody has ever been sane enough to try his way," wrote George Bernard Shaw (in the preface to *Androcles and the Lion*).

JESUS AS ONE WHO
LOVED HIS ENEMIES

In both Matthew and Luke, Jesus' response to his opposition is to withdraw for regrouping and renewal of his energies. In addition he gathered disciples and began to forge a weapon, the ultimate weapon, which he was to use with such great effectiveness, namely, the parable.

One perspective from which to view the parables is as a weapon of confrontation. The parable was not invented by Jesus. It is found in the Old Testament, particularly in the brilliant story that Nathan told David the prophet (2 Sam. 12:2–4). And yet in the use of the parable, once David had rendered the verdict "That man deserves to die," the hammer of condemnation came down in such a way that David could not escape. He is pinned down by his own verdict, condemned by his own words. Nathan's parable catches David in his own sense of justice and fairness. But the parable appeals to David's conscience and respects his humanity by allowing him to come to his own conclusion. His own insight allows him to come to accountability, but he remains free to draw his own conclusion.

While the parables of Jesus also have a remarkable way of calling people to account for their own actions, they do not as directly condemn people. Nor is Jesus ever described as using the words of Nathan "you are the man" (2 Sam. 12:7). The reason for this would seem to be that in the way that Jesus told his stories, his opponents were always allowed room to maneuver. They were always free to reject the story as not applying to them or as being irrelevant to their style of life. What they could not do was to avoid the question posed by the parable.

When Jesus used the parable as a tool of confrontation, he was totally consistent with the "love your enemies" teaching. If he had not loved his enemies, he would not have told them stories. Telling them stories gave them an opportunity to reexamine themselves, to assess the way in which they lived, to get caught up in the stories and by being caught up in them, brought closer to the graciousness, mercy, and love of God.

Had Jesus been a quietist, he would have withdrawn to an Essene monastery. Had he been a pacifist, he would have spent his whole life and ministry denouncing war and describing why people should not participate in it. Jesus was neither of those. He was instead a peace-maker who forged weapons of peace in such a way that he could express his love to those who were God's and his enemies. He did this in a manner which affirmed their dignity as human beings by allowing them free choice.

The parable is the highest compliment paid to Jesus' enemies because it was an appeal to their intellect and allowed them freedom to choose. He treated his enemies as people who could respond to the gracious drawing of God. That is what it means to love your enemies.

Even if it could be shown that on one or two occasions Jesus was rude to his enemies, it is clear that the overall picture of Jesus offered us by the gospels is of one who lived fully for others. To be sure he rebuked his mother (John 2:4), called Peter's suggestion inspired by Satan (Mark 8:33), and does not really conform to the picture of a gentle, meek and mild Jesus. His anger shows at times (Mark 1:41; 3:5), but overall his anger is directed at situations and not at people in such a way that they are crushed.

In the passion narratives it becomes clear that Jesus called even Judas his friend. In Matthew's account of the arrest of Jesus, Judas is addressed as: "Friend, do what you have come to do" (26:50, au. trans.). The address, "Friend," appears two more times in Matthew (20:13; 22:12) and stresses on each occasion the relationship which exists between two parties. Matthew's bias against Judas leads him to mention the fact that Judas is expressing that relationship in an aberrant way. Nevertheless one cannot escape the gentleness and the warmth of Jesus' treatment of Judas during their final encounter.

It is consistent with Jesus' approach to his enemies that even his disciples who betray and deny him are treated with utmost gentleness, without any rebuke whatever. The Gospel writers seem to have missed the fact that Jesus was prepared to be the ultimate scapegoat. They began the long Christian tradition of making Judas the scapegoat or the villain. The evidence leads us to the conclusion that Jesus loved his enemies throughout his life. No rebuke of Judas ever passes his lips, and in his dealings with all of the authorities, he is a model of the righteous one who suffers for others.

Consistent with this picture, Luke portrays Jesus as the one who, in the midst of great pain and agony on the cross, thought about the welfare of those responsible for putting him there, as well as the welfare of those who mocked him as he hung dying. Thus the prayer, "Father forgive them; for they know not what they do" (Luke 23:34), one of two sayings from the cross which Luke records, becomes for him the parallel to the words of Socrates that he bore no malice towards those who condemned him to his death (*Apology* 41). Jesus, however, goes one step further and prays for his enemies. Without in any way minimizing the enormity of their sin, he prays that God will find a way to forgive them. To the one who is crucified alongside of him, Jesus also promises that he will join him in paradise even though he too had mocked him with the words: "Are you not the Christ? Save yourself and us" (Luke 23:39; cf. Mark 15:32; Matt. 27:44).

It is important that we do not confuse the issue here. Jesus does not forgive his enemies. To offer forgiveness to those who are not interested in it, is always to cheapen forgiveness. The triumph of his spirit of love is to request of God that in some way he may grant forgiveness. How different this is from those who curse their executioners, those who pray that God may reward them adequately for their deed, and those who in the hour of death are so overwhelmed by their own pain, suffering, and the darkness which they face, that they cannot think of others. Even if it were proved that Jesus never spoke those words on the cross, it could still be argued that his whole life was a prayer of forgiveness on behalf of those who opposed God in manifold ways. At any rate, for Luke and his readers it is clear that Jesus stands as part of the great tradition in the Hellenistic world of people who were able to take their enemies seriously, be benevolent toward them, and in the end intercede on their behalf to God.

Whether Luke and Matthew give us a totally reliable picture of Jesus in this respect is then beside the point. What is clear is that this picture of Jesus emerged in the first century and with great momentum carried the church into the Greco-Roman world. He taught his disciples to love their enemies and practiced that teaching himself. This was seen by the early church as the greatest contribution to peace in their world. It is no wonder that Luke summarizes the work of Jesus as the "good news of peace" (Acts 10:36), for he sees in Christ's Lordship, especially as it is expressed through the coming to faith of non-Jews, the wholeness which humankind needs to survive.

At the same time Luke reports that Jesus' great expectations for bringing peace to his own people were frustrated by their unwillingness to listen to him and to accept his way of peace. Thus Jesus weeping over the city of Jerusalem before his final confrontation with the authorities is the cry of a prophet who finds that the people will reject him as God's word. "If only you had known, on this great day, the way that leads to peace!" (Luke 19:42, NEB). Because the authorities do not, they will pay for their disobedience through the destruction of their beautiful city, their religious institutions, and the lives of innocent women and children.[20]

THE DISCIPLES AS CHILDREN
OF PEACE

Consistent with Luke's portrait of Jesus as a peace bringer, he portrays Jesus as commissioning his disciples to go forth into Galilee and gather together the children of peace (Luke 10:1–10). Some elements of this portrait deserve special comment:

1. "Behold, I am sending you out as lambs in the midst of wolves" (Luke 10:3; cf. Matt. 10:16). In both Greek and Jewish circles this contrast is well known. It appears in apocalyptic writings where the Jews are portrayed as lambs in the midst of the nations. With reference to the Maccabean struggle, the lamb arises to become the most powerful and is able to throw off all attackers (1 *Enoch* 89:46; cf. T. Joseph 19:8). It does not appear frequently in the New Testament but it could easily go back to Jesus as an arresting warning of the risk which the disciples undertook on that mission or any they might undertake subsequently. At any rate, Jesus is using imagery here which goes back to Sumerian civilization which depicted an ideal primitive time when the wolf and the lamb lived together in peace. Isaiah (11:6) and another writer under his name (65:25) look forward to the time when that will again be possible. The writer of Sirach assumes that the two cannot get along together anymore than the sinner and the devout (13:15–20). Luke has Jesus calling for a total vulnerability, and Matthew attenuates it only slightly by adding: "be wise as serpents and innocent as doves" (10:16). In either case the gentle nature of their mission is stressed. When discussions are held about doves and hawks, wolves and lambs, the follower of Jesus who goes out in his name has no choice. Lambs do not devour; they are devoured. Lambs do not kill; they are killed.

2. The command not to exchange greetings on the road (Luke 10:5). This instruction has created considerable difficulty, and perhaps Matthew already sensed that difficulty and therefore did not include it. A good case has been made for seeing this as a symbolic

protest which would have been so offensive to the ones the disciples met, that it would have had the force of attracting attention in an unmistakable way to the disciples. R. Johanan ben Zakkai is praised for the fact that never did anyone anticipate him with the salutation of peace, not even a heathen in the marketplace (*b.Berakoth* 17a). Only in a place of filth was the greeting forbidden (*Perek Hashalom* 59b, 11). It is as if Jesus here is saying that sometimes the emissaries of peace must withhold the common greeting of peace in order to attract attention to the seriousness of the current situation. Just as the prophets at times engaged in socially shocking symbolic actions (cf. Ezekiel's behaviour in showing how he bears the sins of the people, Ezekiel 4—5) so Jesus instructs his disciples to forego a common courtesy to call attention to their presence. Nevertheless the purpose of their mission is to make peace.[21]

3. Child of Peace. a. "Child of peace" *(ben shalom)* can be the person who has peace. In 2 Sam. 2:7 reference is made to the sons of strength—men who are strong. One could compare the son of knowledge—the one who possesses knowledge, or the sons of Haggadah—the ones who possess knowledge of Haggadah.

b. It can also mean "the one destined for peace" or "to whom it is suited." Matthew seems to read it thus when he says, "worthy" of peace (10:11). In Jewish sources the terms "son of the world to come," or "children of Gehenna" refer to future states.

c. A third alternative emerges if the difference between "son of peace" and "man of peace" was blurred (cf. 1 Chron. 22:9 where the phrase "man of peace" is applied to Solomon). The term "man of peace" *(ish shalomi)* appears in Ps. 41:9(10) and is translated by the LXX (40:10) as "a man of my peace." In that case Jesus might be referring to those whom they can trust or who already belong to the inner circle. But this meaning seems far-fetched.[22]

It may be that the formula designates not only belonging to, but also dependence upon; essential relationship to or obligation towards. At any rate, there are many usages of it in Judaism: son of the kingdom (Matt. 8:12), sons of light, sons of darkness, sons of righteousness, sons of Beliar, and so forth.

The term "son of Torah" comes closest perhaps to the term "child or son of Peace." For the son of the Torah is one who dedicates himself to the study of the Torah and in that way becomes one learned in Torah. So it is likely that Jesus, when he asked his disciples to go out to gather the children of peace, was sending them out to identify with those in Galilee who were bent on pursuing peace. Their own commitment to peace was taken for granted.

There is no agreement on the social background of this commission. Paul Hoffmann has argued that the Zealots or proto-Zealot movements are reflected in this mission.[23] As the Zealots called children of rebellion for their battle of liberation of Jerusalem, so Jesus called children of peace. To be sure, Menachem's battle did not begin until the year 66 but there is no reason to assume that the preparations were not already being made during the time of Jesus' ministry, and they certainly must have been very much alive as Luke composed his Gospel. Accordingly Jesus would have asked his disciples to go out two by two to recruit the children of peace. Hoffmann's thesis cannot be established with any certainty, and there are still those who argue that we should not speak of Zealots or a Zealot party until the fifties. It does seem strange that the formula which one would fully expect to find in the first-century Jewish community, in view of the prominence given both to shalom and to the formula "son of . . . ," has not been demonstrated there. It has so far been found only as attributed to Jesus of Nazareth. Why not conclude that he formulated it?

If so we are dealing here with a critical term of normative self-definition. For whereas such terms as "disciple" are defined by the person to whom the disciple is attached, the term "child of peace" has a certain autonomy, a certain distinctness which allows it to stand by itself.

We should not in this instance make an exclusive choice between an objective or subjective genitive. In Hebrew thinking, distinctions between those two are not made as precisely as we might like. This means that the "child of peace" is not only someone who is a product of peace but also is someone who is destined for peace, in short someone for whose total existence *shalom* is the key ingredient. It is the ground of being as well as the goal toward which one moves.

Hoffmann was the first to stress that we are dealing here with a social context in which undoubtedly many others were going out to recruit for various activities. It is highly likely that during the days of Jesus, work was already being done to recruit for resistance against

Rome. The war against Rome (which was to start in the year 66 C.E.), resulting in the terrible destruction of Jerusalem in 70 C.E. and the total annihilation of all Jewish resistance movements in the spring of 74 C.E. at the fall of Masada, was vitally joined to that same resistance movement.

Even if we could be convinced that Jesus makes peace the hallmark of those whom the disciples are to recruit, we must allow for the possibility that the word "peace" was misused as much in those days as it is today. That is why the content that is given to this term and to the mission of the disciples is of critical importance.

Certainly with regard to the structure of Luke's Gospel, the central place which this mission of the disciples holds cannot be ignored. It is as a result of their mission that Jesus is able to be exultant (Luke 10:21), the only time he is described as such in the Gospels, because he has seen the power of Satan broken (10:18). It is as if Jesus now transfers his hopes and his expectations onto his disciples. For with the ominous clouds of opposition gathering around himself, and his own demise becoming more and more inevitable, it is necessary to focus his attention upon those whom he has recruited. Through their ability and the effectiveness of their ministry, Jesus sees that his power and authority can be conveyed to the disciples, leading him to the conviction that the power of the demonic can be broken. Because there are "children of peace," the work of God can go on, and Jesus himself has an occasion for rejoicing.

The way in which this community, the "children of peace," deals with power is abundantly illustrated in Luke's Gospel. Luke has a particular concern about the structure of human relationships and he agrees with the other Gospels in placing the "little people" at the front of Jesus' concerns. More explicitly than the other Gospels, Luke makes it clear that the power structure among the "children of peace" is different. In the final confrontation of Jesus with his disciples— where John describes the incident of the feet washing and the towel (13:14–16) and uses that as his means of illustrating the power structure in the community—Luke has Jesus say that he "confers upon them" the kingdom (22:28–30) and expects them to rule in the kingdom of God in the way that he has shown them. This method of ruling eliminates the power struggle and sets its highest premium on the way in which one serves the neighbor.

JESUS AND THE ZEALOTS

There has been considerable discussion recently about Jesus and his relationship to the revolutionary party of the Zealots. There is unanimity that the Zealots were a force to be reckoned with at the time of Jesus, although some argue that they emerged as a "party" in the years after 60 C.E. Much of this discussion has been clouded by the attempt to put a degree of precision into the use of terms by Josephus. The search for Jesus' own attitude is confused by contemporary agendas to align Jesus more closely with the revolutionary struggle of our time.

Those who accept the genuineness of Jesus' teaching of "love your enemies" cannot argue that he was a Zealot. Everything that we know of Zealot ideology runs counter to the doctrine of loving the enemy. According to the Zealots, the enemy (particularly the collaborator, who is outwardly a member of the Jewish people but collaborates with Rome or other "demonic powers") becomes a target of God's holy wrath. The wrath is expressed through the Zealot himself who becomes the agent of God's wrath and is under a mandate to kill those who have not maintained God's purity. Appeals are made to the Old Testament (Gen. 34:25–29), Moses and the Levites (Exod. 32:26–29), Elijah (1 Kings 18—19), and Mattathias (1 Macc. 2:24).

The Zealot model of behavior par excellence is Phinehas who in Numbers 25 is described as having the courage to intervene and kill Zimri who violated the divine commandment by taking a Midianite woman (see above pp. 45–47). For this, Phinehas is rewarded as the one who established the covenant of peace. This covenant of peace (25:12–13)[24] *in perpetuum* gives to Phinehas the prominence that he has in later Jewish literature even into the first century.[25] He is commended for acting with God's own zeal (v. 11) and for thus performing atonement (v. 13).

This model of atonement is one that obviously had great attraction for some first-century Jews. As recently as 1980 Menachem Begin, when asked about Moses, discounted him as a weak man "forced to rely upon his nephew Phinehas to take the initiative in stemming the tide of intermarriage" (*New York Times,* October 5, 1980). According to some it was particularly in Galilee that the Zealots had a strong hold, but in any case it is clear that Jesus, given his love for the law, would have been attracted by this historical antecedent and this model of making atonement in the history of Israel. It is highly probable that John the Baptist saw Phinehas as a messianic model and that he expected Jesus to embody that. His message (Luke 3:7–9) fits with Malachi's description and also with traditional interpretations of Phinehas' role.

What seems clear from all the evidence we have is that Jesus decisively rejected that model. Instead of Phinehas, Jesus seems to have lived in the spirit of Isaiah or even of Moses who, given the choice between his life and the life of the people, said that God should destroy him rather than the people (Exod. 32:9–14, 32). In this respect Moses, Jesus, and Paul all rejected the assumption that they would become agents of God's vengeance, allowing that matter rather to stay in the hands of God. They were prepared to give up their own lives for their people. It follows that Jesus also decisively rejected the role John the Baptist had announced for him, for the theme of violent judgment is missing from his message.

But did not Jesus have some disciples who were Zealots? There is clear evidence in the gospels that Simon the Zealot (Luke 6:15) was a member of the Twelve. Peter at times displayed Zealot tendencies, as did the "sons of thunder," and perhaps other disciples like Judas Iscariot may have been a member of the Zealot group. To argue, however, that because Jesus had certain disciples who were Zealots, he himself had Zealot tendencies or sympathies, is sophomoric. It would be as wise and as consistent to argue that because certain of his disciples had been prostitutes, Jesus was a pimp, or that he also had a tendency in the direction of sexual prostitution!

The presence of the Zealots among Jesus' disciples clearly indicates that they were attracted to the zeal which Jesus himself manifested. Undoubtedly at times they wished that he would take the alternative of Phinehas and employ his tactics.

On the surface there is no reason to deny that this alternative was very attractive to Jesus himself. Could it not be the case that the biggest difficulty Jesus had was to make his selection from the models of behavior presented to him in the Old Testament? The models of Isaiah and Phinehas could not be more disparate. Who is to say that one is God's way for Jesus whereas the other is not? Undoubtedly, the Gospels in the temptation narratives, as well as in the Gethsemane account, indicate that Jesus had to make very difficult choices, that he could not simply take one portion of the Hebrew Scriptures as a guide, but that in every respect he had to come to terms with the diversity in the Scriptures and above all the models for atonement and reconciliation which they presented to him.

What the Gospels indicate is that Jesus wrestled his way through to a decision on that matter. They show consistently a picture of Jesus as the Suffering Servant and as one who did not retreat from conflict with evil but confronted it in a way that was in harmony with God's will. Specifically he rejected holy war, at least one in which disciples kill others, as a tactic to bring in the kingdom.

But were there not certain instances when Jesus did not follow the way of Isaiah but the way of the Zealots? Much has been made of the cleansing of the temple, of the two swords pericope in Luke 22, and statements like "I have come not to bring peace, but a sword" (Matt. 10:34; cf. Luke 12:51).

His cleansing of the temple, whatever we make of it, must always be compared with the manner used by Menachem, the Zealot, some thirty-three years later (66 C.E.) in which the chief priest was murdered. There is in any case considerable evidence that the transaction of business in sacrificial objects had been newly introduced and that Jesus was not alone in his opposition to this practice.

The Gospels vary considerably in recounting this event. The Synoptic Gospels refer to the temple as a house of prayer and not a den of robbers (Matt. 21:13; Mark 11:17; Luke 19:46) with Luke having the least interest in the incident and all synoptics make no reference to animals (Matthew and Mark mentioning the doves). John is the only one to refer to the animals as if to justify the hastily made whip. The Fourth Gospel is the only one to mention "zeal" as part of the motivation for the act (2:17; see below n. 29).

The act itself serves as a powerful illustration that Jesus did intervene for the disadvantaged at some risk and that he did not adopt a stoical approach to evils around him. That the incident is so often cited by moderns to justify the violence of terrorism and armed struggle points up the poverty of our understanding of the way in which Jesus dealt with evil. At the very most one might appeal to it as a method for cleaning out God's place of prayer. If you are going to release bulls in a public place, a whip is essential to keep them from trampling on bystanders. As a farm boy I can appreciate the need for a whip to control bulls. The fact that Jesus hastily made a whip from the cords which bound the animals, far from indicating that he had lost his cool and was prepared to begin thrashing the merchants, indicates rather his profound respect for all the people there and his desire to protect them from the trampling of the bulls. As every farm boy can tell you, a whip can control bulls, and John notes with some surprise that having made the whip he cast them all out, both the sheep and the bulls (John 2:15). Presumably the sheep did not need the whip. Just because the artists have enjoyed portraying this scene as Jesus whipping the merchants does not mean that we should distort the text or take a practice from a shepherd and justify preparation for a nuclear war!

The incident in the temple may have had messianic connotations for those standing around, but it was hardly seen as an action which transformed Jesus, from a person who had never coerced anyone before, into a Zealot revolutionary. It had best be seen as a symbolic act in line with what so many prophets of the Old Testament did in order to get their point across, an act which, however, also caused the prophets considerable trouble.

THE TWO SWORDS

One of the most difficult pericopes is Luke 22:35–38. In it Jesus asks his disciples whether they have ever lacked anything in their previous missions when they went out "barefoot without purse or pack." When they reply "No," he says:

> It is different now, . . . whoever has a purse had better take it with him, and his pack too; and if he has no sword, let him sell his cloak to buy one. For Scripture says, "And he was counted among the outlaws," and these words, I tell you, must find fulfilment in me; indeed, all that is written of me is being fulfilled. "Look, Lord," they said, "we have two swords here." "Enough, enough," he replied (NEB).

The history of interpretation of this passage cannot detain us now. We can join in the unanimous current opinion that Luke is clearly not depicting this event as support for those who felt that for Christians to survive they must be armed for self-protection or offensive action. This would be to subvert everything else that Luke records about the nature of Christ's kingdom. Also it is clear from Luke 22:49–51 that

Jesus does not endorse the use of the sword by his disciples to protect him.

Rather the key to the meaning of the incident appears in Jesus' final reply: "Enough of this kind of talk." Clearly they did not grasp the meaning of his words of warning, and the violent metaphor Jesus used on this occasion missed the mark. For us it is more important to grasp what the text *does not* mean even when we cannot reconstruct the original setting of the saying or its application to Luke's contemporaries. "Our narrator, in speaking of the sword, was not thinking of an accommodation to the 'Worldly kings' who take the sword to protect their majesty. Jesus separated himself and his followers totally from them by going to the cross."[26] He went to that cross not like a Zealot cursing his executioners but praying for their salvation instead. Clearly this text cannot be used to argue that Jesus urged his disciples to be armed or even to suggest that he was checking on their armaments here.[27] The conclusion argues against that.

NOT PEACE BUT A SWORD

The statement, "I have not come to bring peace, but a sword" (Matt. 10:34; cf. Luke 12:51–52 "division" for "sword") likewise is meant to avoid any shallow notion of peace. Jesus does not let matters run on as they have in the past. His coming causes upheaval because decisions will have to be made, new loyalties will form, and this will be disruptive. "The true saints are those who transfer the state of householdership to the house of God, becoming father and mother, brother and sister, son and daughter, to all creation, rather than to their own issue"[28] and that transfer cannot be made easily. From the time of Tyrtaeus of Greece, through the call of the Levites in Israel, to the Cynics, Essenes, and even some Stoics it was made clear by many great teachers that the struggle for ultimate values leads often and perhaps always through the division which cuts like a sword into the very heart of the family. In this respect Jesus is not an exception but rather takes his place alongside of all great religious leaders. To assume that such an affirmation makes him a Zealot or someone dedicated to change through violence, and therefore not a peacemaker, is absurd.

All of these incidents must be looked at carefully and taken with utmost seriousness. In the cleansing of the temple it is clear that Jesus is angry that the temple, for example, has been misused for purposes other than its original intention.[29] There is no doubt that in this instance he acts as an aggressive reformer who is prepared to upset the economic values of the people involved, take the risks of animals trampling over human beings, and violate certain canons of private property in pursuit of a higher goal.

It may even be, as traditionally portrayed, that Jesus used coercion in this instance. But if so, it can hardly be used as a prototype to invalidate all of his other teachings on peace. It is the best illustration of a "militant nonviolent" tactic. The overall impression of his ministry clearly indicates that he used persuasion and the word rather than a sword. Certainly the incident cannot be used to justify armed intervention, guerrilla warfare, or arming of liberation movements, as has been the case in the recent past. The incident can be used to justify intervention where injustices are being perpetrated, but that intervention must be consistent with the goals toward which Christian groups are working.

Jesus is a revolutionist in that he attacked violence at its roots. As the Gospel of John already indicates, he is one who gives a kind of peace which is alien to the world's understanding. He gives peace but not as the world thinks, which is that it can bring peace by making war. It is wrong to assume that the peace which he brings has nothing to do with the state of nations and their relations to each other. It does include that but provides a deeper basis in that it is built upon relations between people, is based on justice, and stresses not merely the absence of external conflict but also wholeness where people are valued for what they are and what God intends for them to become. Above all it is a state in which no one is coerced into behavior which does not come from the will. For a society which is based on coercion is nothing less than an armed camp, a powder keg, which awaits only the appropriate time until it explodes.

Jesus was never called the "Prince of Peace" in the New Testament. Nevertheless the early Christians acknowledged him as their Lord and as their Peace. This means that any involvement by Christians in peace is natural and normal. It is not motivated by fear, panic or frustration. For the Christian to work for peace is as normal as to pray, to partake in the Eucharist or to acknowledge Jesus as Lord. It is more normal than to recite the Creed. The Christian commitment to peace springs from that joy which is a direct result of union with Christ. That which has been received without our merit we also freely share with others.

Finally, to be a follower of Jesus today means to go outside the camp. People like to place us in certain camps and put labels like doves, hawks, pacifists and so forth on us. But just when we think that we have a person labelled as a pacifist, we discover that there is a militant nonviolence in that person which surprises us. People have tried very hard to describe Jesus as a pacifist. But he makes no grand statements opposing war. He has also been appealed to by terrorists. He is bigger than both. He commands his disciples to love their enemies. A disciple is left then with the problem: Can I love my enemy if I shoot to kill him? Do I love my enemy if I ignore him?

We do not capture the message of Jesus with terms like "nonviolence" or "pacifism." He had a positive, militant, but nonviolent, message. He announced the kingdom of God as present. In it the children of peace had found a community in which their Lord would direct a campaign for gathering together those who pray for peace, speak for peace, work for peace, and, if necessary, with Jesus die for peace. That army for peace has marched for nearly twenty centuries and marches still. If we look carefully we can see that Jesus still leads that group even though at times there are great difficulties in discerning his orders behind the cries of many leaders and over the din of confusing orders and the screaming of many bombers and bullets.

No Gospel writer so clearly stresses the importance of peace in the work of Jesus as does Luke. He draws together the command to love the enemy with the prospect of peace. Furthermore, he reports that Jesus consistently loved his enemies even to the point of praying for them while he was dying on the cross. If we wish to know the way to peace and if we want the cloud of death to be removed from us, we must be prepared to listen to what Luke has to tell us. He lived like we in a world where many people cried "peace" and many proposed alternative paths to peace. Luke bridged the gap between Jew and Gentile, between rich and poor, between educated and uneducated. He saw that in the way in which Jesus lived, his openness to sinners and the "little folk" like women, children, Samaritans, publicans, and the like, a path was broken which could lead to peace. In this respect, we shall see later, Luke's picture of Jesus is similar to Paul's.

PEACE AS A GIFT FROM GOD:
FOURTH GOSPEL

There is in the early Christian community a firm conviction that the gift of Jesus to the world is peace. We have already observed it in the annunciation of the birth of Christ in Luke's Gospel. John's Gospel has its own way of expressing this when in the farewell discourse (14:27–28) Jesus says:

> Peace I leave with you; my peace I give to you; not as the world gives do I give to you. Let not your hearts be troubled, neither let them be afraid.

The primary reference point for this peace is not absence of conflict, for the peace of Jesus always sets him and his disciples against the world. It is going too far, however, when Raymond Brown asserts: "The peace of which Jesus speaks has *nothing* to do with the absence of warfare"[30] (my italics). As he himself notes, peace has to do with the hope that the messiah will bring peace to the nations (Zech. 9:10), and if the peace of Christ is equated with the gift of eternal life and joy then surely "absence of warfare" cannot be bracketed out. Nor can one exclude the inner peace, for John's Gospel has Jesus saying in 16:33,

> I have said this to you, that in me you may have peace. In the world you have tribulation [trouble], but be of good cheer, I have overcome [conquered] the world.

Surely one constricts too narrowly the mission of Christ to rule out any possibility that through this mission, he believed he brought an opportunity to end potentially the warring of peoples against each other. At the very least, the Fourth Gospel affirms that those who follow Jesus also take their place as peacemakers in the world, even as they state the oneness with each other, which in the Fourth Gospel seems integral to their mission (17:11).

Three times the risen Christ appears among his followers and declares his peace to them (20:19, 21, 26). If we agree that this has a profoundly religious dimension (used with "grace" as a standard Christian greeting in the letters of the early church), it may also be assumed that categorically to rule out the absence of warfare in this definition of peace is to give it a meaning contrary to any found in the literature of the time. Peace for the Fourth Gospel means more, much more than absence of warfare. It would be folly to assume that it *includes* warfare as that term is generally used. The victory of Christ which he achieved and which is available to his disciples is a victory over evil and violence, including the way the world wages war. Like all of Christ's gifts, this wholeness is an eschatological gift available to all who wish to receive it and live in its new found freedom to love even the enemy.

What is important in John 16:33 is that the peace of Christians is something which they have in Christ: "*in me* you have peace." In the world the normal state of the Christian is trouble. But the Christian finds norms in Christ and while troubles may stem from that clash between the Christ and the values of the world, the Christian is at peace. That peace stems from the fact that Christ has won the victory (conquered—a military term) over the world. (Cf. 16:33b, NEB: "The victory is mine; I have conquered the world.") Therefore the admonition to take heart or have courage.

The one who follows Christ then partakes in the victory which Christ has already achieved. Naive ignorance of the evils of the world, innocence with respect to the harm the enemy can inflict, do not characterize the Christian. The courage of the Christian flows from the knowledge of being in Christ, the world conqueror himself. Because that one has won the victory, the Christian is free to refuse to engage in worldly warfare. To do otherwise is to live as if Christ had not conquered the powers.

The New Testament writers do not lay much stress on the classical military virtue of courage. Rather they insist that courage comes to us as we take our position with Christ the victor and participate in his victory over evil, death, and disease. Each time a New Testament writer uses the words, "Be of good cheer" or "Take courage" he does so in virtue of what God is about to do or has already done in Jesus Christ (see Matt. 9:2; 22 variant reading; 14:27; Acts 23:11). Thus, they stress not only the importance of the courage to be but rather the courage to be in Christ and to live by his power. The Greek might screw up his courage, thinking that beyond this world lay a better existence where he was freed from the tomb which was the body. The Christian, like the Jew, took courage from the conviction that God would act through his people *within* history. For it was within history that God has redeemed his people from slavery, and it was within the first century ambiguities of history that God had acted decisively to free humankind from the terror of war. Without this repeated stress on the victory of Christ, all talk of peace makes no sense. The early Christian community did not cower in the shadows. They were propelled into the cities and villages of the Roman Empire in the strong conviction that no foe could vanquish them for none had vanquished their Lord. Only such a conviction rekindled in our time will lead us to act decisively to avoid a suicidal war which will destroy us all. Fear can be overcome. It is still the mightiest generator of conflict and fuels our current arms race. For Christians to become a part of this hysteria is to fail in their faith in Jesus and is to deny him as the "Prince of Peace." We must avoid it at all costs and can do so as we live fully in the reality which is "Christ the Conqueror."

NOTES

1. New light has been cast upon the Jewish revolutionary movements and terrorist groups which existed in the first century. S. G. F. Brandon argued that Jesus had deeper affinities with this movement than the gospel writers (because of their pacific sympathies) allow us to see (*Jesus and the Zealots* [Manchester: Manchester Univ. Press, 1967]). For an opposite point of view see Martin Hengel, *Was Jesus a Revolutionist?* (Philadelphia: Fortress Press, 1971) and *Victory Over Violence: Jesus and the Revolutionists* (Philadelphia: Fortress Press, 1973).

2. On the saying, "Love your enemies" which is taken here as integrally related to the quest for peace and as a concrete way of peacemaking, it has been unanimously asserted that it goes back to Jesus himself ("If anywhere we can find what is characteristic of the preaching of Jesus," Rudolf Bultmann, *History of the Synoptic Tradition* [New York: Harper & Row; Oxford: Blackwell, 1968], 105). See also Walter Bauer, "Das Gebot der Feindesliebe und die alten Christen," *ZTK* 27 (1917): 37–54; Herbert Braun, *Radikalismus* (Tübingen: J. C. B. Mohr, 1957) II: 91 n. 2; Dieter Lührmann ("Liebet eure Feinde" *ZTK* 69 [1972]: 412–38): "It can be affirmed with the greatest certainty available to exegesis that these words belong to Jesus himself" (412). See further Paul Minear, *Commands of Christ* (Nashville: Abingdon Press, 1972), Chap. 4; W. C. van Unnik, "Die Motivierung der Feindesliebe in Lukas 6:32–35," *NovT* 8 (1966): 284–300; Luise Schottroff, "Non-Violence and the Love of One's Enemies," in *Essays on the Love Commandment*, ed. R. Fuller (Philadelphia: Fortress Press, 1978), 9–39. Piper, *"Love Your Enemies,"* 1, 58, cf. 64–65. The way in which Norman Perrin treated this saying of Jesus (*Rediscovering the Teaching of Jesus* [New

York: Harper & Row; London: SCM Press, 1967] 39, 148) is judiciously but convincingly criticized by Minear (*Commands of Christ,* 80–81). Once it had been granted that these words go back to Jesus scholars like Norman Perrin lost interest. We are apparently so absorbed with exploring the criteria of genuineness that we neglect the much bigger challenge of trying to ascertain what it means to *do* what Jesus taught.

3. Following Roy Harrisville (*The Miracle of Mark* [Minneapolis: Augsburg Pub. House, 1967]) the Gospel of Mark is a commentary on the humiliation exaltation motif expressed in Phil. 2:5–11, basic to early Christian concepts of the Messiah's peacemaking role.

4. Johannes Wilkens, *Der König Israels,* 2 vols. (Berlin: Furche Verlag, 1934, 1937).

5. I am indebted here in particular to Hans Windisch, "Friedensbringer-Gottessöhne. Eine religionsgeschichtliche Interpretation der 7. Seligpreisung" *ZNW* 24 (1925): 240–60 and to the important article "Herrscherkult und Friedensidee" in *Umwelt des Urchristentums,* ed. J. Leipoldt and W. Grundmann (Berlin: Evangelischer Verlagsanstalt, 1965), 127–42. Trygaeus, thanks to his ascension to heaven by riding on a dung beetle and rescue of Peace, is proclaimed as "Saviour of all men" in Aristophanes' *Peace.*

6. As Erik Erikson puts it: "Nonviolent behavior must often be shocking in order to shake up the violent opponent's seemingly so normal attitude, to make him feel that his apparently undebatable and spotless advantage in aggressive initiative is being taken away from him and that he is being forced to overdo his own action absurdly" ("The Galilean Sayings and the Sense of 'I'," *The Yale Review* 70 [1981]: 357). David Balch called my attention to this important article.

7. Ragnar Höistad, *Cynic Hero and Cynic King: Studies in the Cynic Conception of Man* (Uppsala, 1948) pursues this aspect from earliest Greek times to the time of the New Testament as he looks at various aspects of the Cynic perception of man. See Jose Miranda (*Marx and the Bible* [Maryknoll, N.Y.: Orbis Books, 1974], 128–29) on Matthew's distinctive use of Isaiah.

8. "Christian scholars have dealt harshly with the Pharisees. There is no doubt a grain of truth in their charges. The Pharisees were dominated primarily by their conviction that the domination of the Jews by religion was an effective means of educating them in the spirit of the Law and thus preparing them for the kingdom of the Messiah." See A. Schalit, ed., *Political History of Jewish Palestine from 332 B.C.E.–67 C.E.* (Jerusalem: Massada Pub. Co., 1972), 291.

9. As suggested by David Flusser and a number of others. The complexity of the matter is evident from John Bowker's *Jesus and the Pharisees* (Cambridge: Cambridge Univ. Press, 1973) who provides data on how difficult it is to define a Pharisee in the first century. Alongside it one must read Sean Freyne, *Galilee From Alexander the Great to Hadrian* (Wilmington, Del.: Michael Glazier, 1980) which does not make it easier to defend the

thesis that Jesus would have been more at home with the Pharisaism of Galilee.

10. W. Klassen, "'A Child of Peace' (Luke 10:6) in First Century Context," *NTS* 27 (1981): 448–506 and John Donahue, "The Good News of Peace," *The Way* 22 (1982): 88–99. See also Willard Swartley, "Politics or Peace in Luke's Gospel," in *Political Issues in Luke-Acts,* ed. R. J. Cassidy and P. J. Scharper (Maryknoll, N.Y.: Orbis Books, 1983), 18–37.

11. Raymond Brown, *The Birth of the Messiah* (Garden City, N.Y.: Doubleday & Co., 1977), 427.

12. Although Brown does draw some interesting parallels and concludes that Luke "claims that the real peace of the world was brought by Jesus" (ibid., 415). An extremely helpful presentation of this aspect appears in Lloyd Gaston's *No Stone on Another,* NovTSup. 23 (Leiden: E. J. Brill, 1970), especially the section, "The Promise of Peace and the Threat of War," 334–65. This solid book has been neglected too much by scholars.

13. See W. Monselewski, *Der barmherzige Samariter* (Tübingen: J. C. B. Mohr, 1967). Among those who have seen this are E. Stauffer, J. Jeremias, Matthew Black, and C. Spicq; see Monselewski, *Samariter,* 138–81.

14. G. B. Caird, "The Transfiguration," *ExpTim* 67 (1955–56): 293–94. Research into the theology of the Samaritans has shown that vengeance was a matter of some theological importance for them. Conversely Jesus seems to have avoided it whenever he could and even on occasions when he might have simply finished a quotation from the Old Testament (e.g., Luke 4:18). The day of vengeance is a concept which seems to have held little attraction for him. On the importance of vengeance for the Samaritans, see John MacDonald, *The Theology of the Samaritans* (London: SCM Press, 1964), 280–90.

15. Helmut Koester, *Synoptische Ueberlieferungen bei den apostolischen Vätern* (Berlin: Akademie Verlag, 1957) indicates that it is the most cited commandment and belonged to the general knowledge of Christians of the day, even those who had never read a gospel (44, 76). He also notes that Polycarp's admonition to pray for enemies probably goes back to the liturgical practice of the church (119).

16. For this interpretation, see Hans Bruppacher, "Was sagte Jesus in Matthäus 5:48?" *ZNW* 58 (1967): 10. He suggests that Aramaic, if pointed in a different way, could well be translated: "you shall retaliate as your heavenly father retaliates." Not a letter needs to be changed to arrive at this interpretation and he appeals to both Walter Baumgartner and another Hebraist, J. Hausherr, in support of his thesis. Ernst Fuchs has argued that the text calls for a self-consciousness which has the strength to love one's enemies. *Telios* stresses a special maturity or self-understanding. If the stress is on maturity or adulthood then the meaning is very close to the Hebrew equivalent (E. Fuchs, "Die vollkommene Gewissheit," in *NT Studien für Rudolf Bultmann,* ed. W. Eltester [Berlin: Walter de Gruyter, 1954], 130–36).

17. The imperative "love" appeals to the will not to the emotions. It calls for action which will contribute to the welfare of the enemy and to his reconciliation with God and man. It is therefore a deeply missionary or evangelical act meant to open the enemy to God's gracious influences after words have failed. The fact that "enemies" is plural is not to be ignored, for there is a constant temptation to assume that it is only the personal enemy which is meant here. It would be a neat trick if one could exempt the religious and political or national enemy from this command. The original does not provide such an easy escape.

18. See Erikson, "Galilean Sayings" (n. 6 above) and also Rollo May, *Power and Innocence* (New York: W. W. Norton, 1972), 20.

19. Peter Stuhlmacher says: "In the light of the recent political situation in which we are placed their way (those who have opposed war) does not appear to me as utopian as a few years ago. It could in fact be that the early church, the fathers of the church, and these little groups have sustained a practice and practiced ahead of time something which today not only Christians but also all mankind needs" ("Aggression, Friede und Versöhnung," in *Das Wort und die Wörter: Festschrift für Gerhard Friedrich,* ed. H. R. Balz, and S. Schulz (Stuttgart: Kohlhammer, 1973), 217. Most theologians have tried to find a way around these hard sayings of Jesus. One discovered that the point of it all was that we should shoot for the lowest common denominator since it all stands under the rubric: Judge not that you be not judged. See Ernst Lerle, "Realisierbare Forderungen der Bergpredigt?", *Kerygma und Dogma* 16 (1970): 32–40. Jack Sanders even promises us that we will appreciate Jesus more if we bear in mind that he does not provide a valid ethic for today (*Ethics in the New Testament* [Philadelphia: Fortress Press, 1978], 29).

20. Joseph Comblin, *Theologie des Friedens* (Vienna: Styria Verlag, 1963), 255ff. "Human peace and Kingdom of God are the two sides of one and the same event" (255).

21. See Iris Bosold, *Pazifismus und prophetische Provokation: Das Grussverbot Lk, 10, 4b und sein historischer Kontext* (Stuttgart: Katholisches Bibelwerk, 1978), 59, 91ff.

22. See my essay "'Child of Peace'" referred to in n. 10 above, esp. 496–97. The article on "ben," *TDOT* II (1975): 153, provides a very good classification.

23. Paul Hoffmann, *Studien zur Theologie der Logienquelle,* NTAbh. 8; Münster: Aschendorff, 1972, 293–334. Luise Schottroff, *Der Sieg des Lebens: Biblische Traditionen einer Friedenspraxis* (Munich: Chr. Kaiser, 1982), 23–47 has an excellent popular treatment of this material.

24. *berith shalom* a singular expression! (cf. Isa. 54:10; Ezek. 34:25, 26).

25. He is always praised in biblical writings. See above, pp. 45–47, and also the considerable material on Phinehas and his influence upon the developments within Judaism during the centuries immediately preceding Jesus in

V. Aptowitzer, *Parteipolitik der Hasmonäerzeit* (Berlin: Kohut-Foundation, 1927).

26. Adolf Schlatter, *Die beiden Schwerter* (Gütersloh: Bertelsmann, 1916), 60. See the detailed study by H. W. Bartsch, "Jesu Schwert-wort, Lukas XXII. 35–38. Überlieferungsgeschichtliche Studie." *NTS* 20 (1974): 190–203. He concludes that no justification for the use of violence is to be found here but also no judgment over the "have-nots" who do use it (202).

27. Brandon, *Jesus and the Zealots,* 16, 340.

28. E. Erikson, *Gandhi's Truth* (New York: Wm. Norton, 1969), 399.

29. The best study of this recorded event is still Jean Lasserre, "Un Contresens Tenace," in *Cahiers de la Reconciliation* (Paris, October 1967) No. 10. See the English summary in his book, *War and the Gospel* (Scottdale, Pa.: Herald Press, 1962), 45–49. Victor Eppstein, "The Historicity of the Gospel Account of the Cleansing of the Temple," *ZNW* 55 (1964): 42–58 points out that the establishment of the transaction of business in sacrificial objects inside the Temple was introduced in the spring of 30 C.E. by Caiaphas. He therefore treats the event as historical, with Jesus taking action possibly the same week it was introduced.

30. R. E. Brown, *The Gospel According to John XIII—XXI,* Anchor Bible (Garden City, N.Y.: Doubleday & Co., 1970), 653.

CHAPTER 5

Paul and the
Good News of Peace

Paul is without doubt the most energetic, articulate, and dynamic leader in the early church. He was a church organizer, an untiring worker, a keen controversialist, a conceptualizer, and not least of all a man who took personal relationships seriously enough so that when peace between human beings was disrupted he sought to restore it. Through his letters we get glimpses into his world of thought. From those sources we shall try to outline his considerable contribution to the early Christian understanding of peace.

From the standpoint of the number of references to peace alone, it is clear that Paul deserves major consideration. The term peace *(eirēnē)* appears some ninety-nine times in the New Testament, being represented at least once in every book except 1 John, in either its verbal or noun form. Of these occurrences, half are found in Paul. When we recall that Paul's writing, including all which have traditionally been attributed to him, comprise only one-fourth of the total writings of the New Testament it becomes clear that peace is an important concept for Paul. Numbers do not tell the whole story although they may point to the need to investigate.

THE PEACE OF CHRIST[1]

Paul's major theological treatise, the Letter to the Romans, is our logical beginning point. It was written to a church which he had not visited and contains an outline of the gospel and its relation to the human predicament. In the first three chapters he presents a formal indictment which leaves all human achievement, even the greatest achievement which God and man have accomplished together—Jewish moral and religious behavior—under God's searing indictment. Slowly and deliberately Paul moves his indictments forward from Rom. 1:20 where he renders this verdict on the first catalogue of sins: "So they are without excuse," no defense for their conduct.

In the second stage he directs his accusation to those who sit in judgment over the wicked and congratulate themselves on their devoutness. "Therefore you have no excuse *(anapologētos)* . . . whoever you are, when you judge another" (Rom. 2:1). In the last stage he concludes that the words of the law are addressed to those who are within the pale of the law, so that no one may have anything to say in self-defense "and the whole world may be held accountable to God" (3:19). With great skill and careful argument Paul has brought humankind to the bar of justice and all that is left is to receive the wrath of God now being revealed from heaven.

But the enormity of human sin and the ineluctability of condemnation has led to an act of God which brought to light his justice—it is something which both prophets and law bear witness to: God's way of righting wrong, effective through faith in Christ (Rom. 3:21–22). Freedom from that indictment can come only through God's act of liberation carried out in Jesus Christ himself according to Rom. 3:25–26 (au. trans.):

> For God designed him to be the means of expiating sin by his sacrificial death, effective through faith. God meant by this to demonstrate his justice, because in his forebearance he had overlooked the sins of the past—to demonstrate his justice now in the present, showing that he is both himself just and justifies anyone who puts their faith in Jesus.

What we have here is similar to Matthew's concern to keep the justice and love of God together. Paul seeks to show that God could look the enormity of human sin fully in the face, note its violation of justice, and yet be reconciled to humankind without destroying it. God allowed Jesus to be killed instead of killing humanity for its sin: a concept of justice which defies all human standards. Human justice demands that when wrong is done, that is, a son killed, then the murderer must pay. Divine justice seems to affirm that even when all of God's prophets are killed, God will go even one step further and send his son into the most vulnerable situation where in fact he will be killed (Luke 20:9–18; Mark 12:1–12; Matt. 21:33–46). Because God does so willingly and voluntarily as a sign of love, reconciliation can take place and justice is done.

This profound miracle of divine love and justice is applied explicitly to peace in Romans 5. A major turning point in Paul's argument takes place as he applies his doctrine of divine justification on the basis of faith to the shape of the Christian life which ensues from its acceptance. In this application peace takes a position of priority.

"Therefore, since we are justified by faith, we have peace with God through our Lord Jesus Christ" (Rom. 5:1). This state of peace exists because the justified ones have entered the sphere of God's grace. Although there are sufferings at present, hope allows the state of exultation. God has flooded the hearts of the believers with his love and this affirms the believer in the conviction that hope is not a mockery.

The strongest evidence of that love is articulated in Rom. 5:6–10:

> While we were still weak [powerless], at the right time Christ died for the ungodly. . . . while we were yet sinners Christ died for us. . . . For if while we were enemies we were reconciled to God by the death of his Son, much more, now that we are reconciled, shall we be saved by his life.

Each of the three references to death stresses that the objects of the death did not deserve the sacrifices being made on their behalf. But the reference which highlights it most is the category of enemy (5:10). All is reinforced by Paul's observation that "one will hardly die for a righteous man—though perhaps for a good man one will dare even to die" (5:7).

One cannot escape the conclusion that in these pregnant lines Paul is offering the theological grounding for his later instructions on how the Roman community is to deal with its enemies (Romans 12). Reconciliation can only come through a sacrificial act of love. Such an act is not determined by the worth of the one for whom one makes the sacrifice. It is grounded only in the love of God and derives both its inspiration and the pattern by which it is expressed equally from God.

That pattern is described explicitly by Paul in 2 Corinthians 5 as a ministry of reconciliation (5:18), a parallel to the ministry of justification mentioned in 2 Cor. 3:9. It is what is later called the "gospel of peace" in the Letter to the Ephesians (6:15). The good news, which those who adhere to Jesus are commissioned to announce, begins with the words that peace is possible between God and his enemies and ends by assuring us that it is also possible between those who accept that gospel and their enemies.

Where does this radical approach come from? We cannot answer that with total certainty. Ernst Käsemann suggested that Paul picked it out of the same tradition from which the author of Ephesians took it: the liturgical tradition (doxology) of the Hellenistic church.[2] According to Käsemann, Paul introduced the theme of atonement, or reconciliation, in order to heighten the notion of the justification of the wicked, as if Paul intensified the concept of justification to include even the justification of the enemies of God. It would seem that Paul must have had some impetus to formulate it this way. Cannot that impetus be found in the life and teaching of Jesus?

He is the one who brought peace, and he is the one through whom the act of reconciliation takes place. The term "reconciliation," as Rudolf Bultmann already observed, points to an even more radical dependence upon God than does the term righteousness of God, "for while the latter means that *without* our doing anything we arrive at 'peace' with God (Rom. 5:1), the former means that *before* any effort of man God made an end of enmity (Rom. 5:10)."[3] For it appears again in that important argument in Romans 8 where Paul describes the two styles of life, that of the flesh which the one who has been united with Christ can leave behind and the new style which is embraced. The new style to which we have been set free has a spiritual orientation: it is life and peace (8:6).

A fundamental definition is provided, and again the word peace appears. Surely we do not do justice to Paul's thought if we restrict this to peace with God, for in Rom. 14:17 the kingdom of God is defined as consisting of peace. In this chapter basic affirmations are being made about the style of the life of freedom in Christ. To be contentious and at enmity is carnal. To recognize that the spirit forms us in the direction of peace and life indicates that both peace and life belong together. Those who reject peace initiate the coming of death.

This theological grounding of Paul's view of peace must be remembered as we turn to that important treatment of this theme in Romans 12, especially in vv. 16–21:

Think of each as equals. Don't consider yourselves lofty, but get carried away with the concerns of little people. Do not keep thinking how clever you are. *Never* pay back evil for evil. Attend to doing good to all. If possible, so far as you can, pursue peace with all people. My dear friends, never carry out revenge yourselves, but make room for divine retribution. For it stands written, "Mine is vengeance; I, myself, will repay," says the Lord. But in the meantime if your enemy is hungry, feed him; if he is thirsty, give him drink. For by doing so you will cause him to change (au. trans.).

PEACE AND THE OUTSIDER
(ROMANS 12)

Although the noun "peace" does not occur in this discussion, the command to live at peace with all does (Rom. 12:18), and the introduction of this theme in Romans 12 is basic to all that Paul says in the last part of that chapter. If we take the theme after v. 9 to be "unhypocritical love within and outside the fellowship" then it is clear that v. 14 shifts the discussion to the outsider.

Bless Those Who Curse[4]

We are dealing with teaching material common to Matthew and Luke on how to deal with an enemy. Paul begins with a word from Jesus: "Call down blessings on your persecutors—blessings, not curses" (Rom. 12:14, NEB). No clue is given to the identity of the persecutors. It is likely that Paul is merely repeating an admonition attributed to Jesus, perhaps one which made a strong impression on him by the fact that when he persecuted the Christians the curse of death he delivered was answered with a blessing (Acts 7:60).

In the "Q" source (Matt. 5:44; Luke 6:28) a similar saying is attributed to Jesus in the context of his command: "Love your enemies." In both Luke and Matthew this is the first illustration of how to love your enemies. When they persecute you (Matthew, Paul) or curse you (Luke 6:28), those who have been reconciled to God through the death of Christ respond with a blessing. It is as if the blessing is the first step in reconciliation. You do not get what you deserve; rather a prayer on your behalf is expressed.

Paul's original text of Rom. 12:14 commands that all persecutors are to be blessed. This, while removing the offensiveness of direct encounter, makes it more impersonal but also makes it more difficult.

Who can speak a blessing on all persecutors, wherever they may be? No wonder Paul's text was altered (between the third and fourth centuries) to read "Bless those who curse *you*" to remove that difficulty. Traditionally you pray "Cursed are all who hate you; blessed for ever will be all who love you" (Tob. 13:12). Paul follows Jesus in prescribing a blessing for those who curse, and it would appear that he makes it even broader by not confining it to those who persecute the Roman community. To my knowledge no English Bible translation has followed the majority of the modern Greek texts which accept the harder reading.

Never Pay Back Evil

The second admonition which speaks directly to the issue of peace is: "Repay no one evil for evil" (Rom. 12:17).[5] It belongs in the same category as "do not return a curse for a curse" and could be considered the general statement. But the idea is ancient and as noted above appears at least as early as Socrates' dialogue with Crito.

One hundred and fifty years before Paul, his fellow Jew, the author of Jubilees, rewrote the events recorded in Genesis 34 and lauded Simeon and Levi for when they slew the Shechemites, Levi is said to have been "zealous to execute righteousness and judgment and vengeance on all those who arose against Israel" (*Jub.* 30:18, 23; Charles, *APOT,* 2:59). Paul takes his stand against all vengeance: He along with many Jews of his day took the position of Socrates.

In addition to his fellow Jews, Paul agreed here with his contemporaries the Stoic, Musonius Rufus and to a lesser degree Epictetus.[6] For both, Socrates was the model to imitate, and although Paul's approach to peace was different than that of the Stoics, the world to which he addressed himself must have been a fertile place for his message.

The Cynics likewise would have provided a fertile soil for his concern for peace. Cynic preachers flourished in the cities and towns in which Paul worked, and recent publication of their writings makes it clear that this dissenting group worked for a world in which narrow provincialism would be overcome and a common humanity would be affirmed which would help all to live at peace with each other.[7] For the Cynic "perfect peace" comes from being freed from every evil through the work of Diogenes "and although we possess nothing, have everything." The Cynics consistently rejected vengeance, for they followed Socrates zealously. Indeed it has been suggested that they lack only Socrates' sense of irony, which among the Cynics has become less courteous.[8] These words of Paul must therefore have been easy for the Romans to comprehend.

Attend to the Good of All

The third admonition which follows is to take heed for the good *(kala)* of all people (Rom. 12:17b). The ancient dictum, "do good to your friends and harm your enemies" is here replaced with a command to try to advance the good not only of your clan and your group but of *all*. In this quote Paul appears to take the idea from Prov. 3:4 but gives it a peculiar twist. Whereas in 2 Cor. 8:21 the two aspects, God and humans, still appear, here the stress is laid only upon *all* people and references to God are deleted. In this way Paul emphasizes the inclusiveness of the love command, for it applies to all, friend and foe, fellow Christian as well as the pagan, who seeks to persecute you. Käsemann notes that the "compound verb is emphatic. Doing good to all is something to be planned and not just willed. . . . Good finds expression in the avoidance of strife and the service of peace. . . ."[9]

Live at Peace with All

The fourth admonition, to live at peace with all (Rom. 12:18), is broader than the command of Jesus given to his disciples, according to Mark 9:50, where it applies to the disciples and their life together. It appears three times in Paul. His earliest use (1 Thess. 5:13) urges peace among believers but also takes in a broader perspective. It appears in connection with the rule: "See to it that no one pays back wrong for wrong, but always aim at doing the best you can for each other and for all" (5:15). Like Rom. 12:16, 1 Thessalonians 5 urges the Christians to encourage the "little people" (5:14, *oligopsychoi*) and support the weak, and to be very patient with all persons. All this is part of living at peace among themselves. Not unrelated is the threefold admonition: "Rejoice always, pray constantly, give thanks in all circumstances; for this is the will of God in Christ Jesus for you" (1 Thess. 5:16–18). Two of them also appear in Romans 12, "Rejoice always" (12:12a and 15a) and "pray constantly" (12:12b). John

Chrysostom shrewdly remarked that only the one who can offer his enemy benevolent love can always rejoice. Both are possible only when sustained by that trust in God which expresses itself in prayer and desires to offer oneself by living according to God's will (Rom. 12:1–2). Proverbs 12:20 affirms that there is "joy with those who give counsels of peace" (JB) or "for those who promote peace" (NIV).

The other reference to living at peace is found in 2 Cor. 13:11 where it applies to the community of believers. The fact that Paul refers to peace three times (2 Cor. 13:11, verb and noun) in this concluding appeal, including once to the kiss of peace, indicates how central he considers it for the existence of the community. Obviously the church cannot contribute to peace in the world if it cannot attain it within its own community. It cannot learn to live at peace with the outside world if it has not learned to do so among those who follow the Prince of Peace.

When Peace Is Broken

Paul's call to live at peace is conditioned by two factors: "As much as it is possible, as far as it lies within your powers" (Rom. 12:18, au. trans.). At times it is impossible to live at peace, not because you don't want to, but because the other party to the conflict desires otherwise. In that case the Christian must examine every action taken in the past or contemplated in the future. Whatever is deliberately provocative must be avoided, and anything which does not promote justice but merely irritates likewise needs to be avoided. The test is clearly the expression of the Lordship of Christ. The Christian cannot discontinue loving his neighbor even if that act of loving irritates others. The Christian cannot hold back simply to retain the semblance of peace. Peace-making may involve irritating people for it challenges their own acts of injustice.

Here, too, Jesus can be a guide. He did not refrain from helping others just because others found it offensive. It is the style of those who follow Jesus as Prince of Peace that they pursue peace with all the powers at their disposal. In doing so they affirm with all their being to everyone that God's love is available to them as well, and that the way of peace is open to them.

It is, however, important to note that Paul does not promise any change will take place in the opponent. The Testament of Benjamin affirms: "If you have a good disposition, even the evil will live at peace with you" (5:1, au. trans.). In the Book of Proverbs it is affirmed that "When a man's ways please the Lord, he makes even his enemies to be at peace with him" (16:7). What these writers affirm is that everyone has a share of the responsibility for keeping the peace. The amount cannot be quantified. It stands to reason, however, that if one side does all in its power to avert conflict or to live at peace, the probability of conflict is at least halved. For conflict feeds on the contribution made by at least *two* and is hard to sustain when one side is committed to living at peace and expresses that commitment. Paul acknowledges that there are limits to what one can do to keep the peace. At the same time he goes beyond that to indicate what the Christian is to do when peace cannot be achieved and conflict breaks out.

When a wrong is done, does vengeance have a place? This is the first question which Paul addresses. His answer is based on Hebrew Scripture, builds upon Greek wisdom, and accords with what enlightened morality had taught for centuries. The rejection of vengeance, in spite of the fact that it flourishes among those not strong enough to resist it, was almost universal among the thinkers of the ancient world. Vengeance was, however, at the basis of Roman law, and the early Greeks saw vengeance as a noble cause.[10]

Paul does not issue a glib rejection of vengeance. The cry for vengeance after all is a human cry. It is a cry which recognizes an injustice. While ruling out every vengeful act, Paul therefore sensitively softens the bluntness of his appeal with the tender address: "Beloved" (Rom. 12:19). It is the only time in the whole letter that Paul addresses the Romans with this emotional word. When grievous wrongs are done and the heart cries out for vengeance, Paul responds with warmth and empathy.

At the same time, the divine law against vengeance stands, and Paul appeals to the Torah of his people. Vengeance is denied humans because there is a place where it occurs and that is in the court of God. "Make room then for God's wrath," (Rom. 12:19, au. trans.) Paul urges, so that it can do its work. How it works has already been abundantly portrayed in the first part of Romans. The Christian can be confident that " 'Vengeance is mine, I will repay' says the Lord" (12:19).

To take vengeance into human hands, then, is to break faith with God. It takes great faith to believe that God is sovereign and will take vengeance in his own way and at his own time. But this is an important affirmation of faith. God does not need us to carry out his acts of vengeance. God alone can see into the heart and judge human acts. To God alone belongs vengeance. We must believe that God will repay. To preempt God's act is to put ourselves in the place of God. It is the ultimate act of unbelief. To be sure, people like the elder brother may not like the way in which the father "punishes" his son (Luke 15). It may be that the father will "punish" the errant son by putting on a party for the son, to welcome him home when he returns from his dissipated living. The elder son, as well, is invited to the party.

The greatest triumph of divine love comes when we get caught up in the celebration of the return to divine love of those who have harmed us in life. Surely the greatest miracle of this love is that we can be transformed in such a way to rejoice not in the destruction of our enemies but in that they are transformed by the love of God which also has transformed us.

Overcoming Evil

Does the Christian then spend time waiting for God's vengeance? Not according to Paul. Rom. 12:20 prescribes the actions available to the Christian in the interim. The "But you, in the mean-time" (*alla* as a strong adversative) charts an alternative course of action. That course of action Paul takes from the book of Proverbs where it stipulates that "If your enemy is hungry, give him bread to eat; and if he is thirsty, give him water to drink" (25:21).

That course of action is striking for a number of reasons. For one thing, it is never included among the several illustrations which Jesus gave about loving the enemy. Nevertheless, it is part of Paul's Jewish heritage found not only in Proverbs but also in such incidents as Elisha delivering a large Syrian army to the king of Israel who is eager to kill them. As noted above, the prophet instructed the king in the art of warfare. He provided a big feast for his enemies and thus averted further raids (2 Kings 6:15–23).

In folk morality the story of Lycurgus of Lacedaemonia was often repeated (see above, pp. 18–19, 25). It would appear, therefore, that unusual as Paul's advice may seem to us, it is clearly taken from Proverbs, which in turn is from Egyptian sources. Closer to the time of Paul we have seen numerous cases in which such an approach was advocated in order to break down enmity.

Paul grounds his admonition as follows (Rom. 12:20b): "For by so doing you will heap burning coals upon his head."[11] The traditional way of interpreting this is to assume that Paul looks forward to severe pain or punishment of the enemy either literally at the time of the final judgment or psychological anguish which will come from pangs of guilt (the dominant position since Augustine).[12] In opposition to that, it has been suggested that an Egyptian repentance ritual in which bearing coals of fire on the head is part of the evidence that reconciliation is desired may have a bearing on this reference to coals of fire (cf. pp. 35–37). Accordingly there would be no reference to pain or agony of any kind since the carrying of coals on the head was a normal way of transporting them at that time. It is argued that any reference to pain inflicted on the enemy in this context, regardless of the purpose of that pain, has to be inferred. It contradicts all that Paul says here about feeding the enemy to keep him alive and about "overcoming evil with good" (Rom. 12:21).

It is important that we recognize the significance of eating and drinking with an enemy. For Paul does not assume, any more than did the writer of the proverb, that you simply hand your enemy some food and offer him/her a drink. Rather, in the Orient one eats and drinks with the one who receives the food. Are we not dealing here with a movement of thought which stressed hospitality as a means of breaking down enmities and avoiding them from coming into being through the virtue of hospitality? Livy stresses this dimension of the law and the practice of hospitality as an alternative to war (Livy 21.2.5), and many others lauded its potential for dealing with xenophobia and affirming the existence of the *humanitas* ideal. Rome, in particular, prided itself by the time of Paul for the way in which the ideal of hospitality was being used to break down barriers that existed between them and strangers as well as enemies. It is hard to think that Paul was not aware of this. In any case he remains closest to his Jewish ethical teaching in what he advises the Romans to do even though the advice would not have been strange to either the Greeks or the Jews who heard these words read.[13]

One of the most thorough studies of this material is provided by John Piper in his book on the love of enemy. His stress on the freedom provided to the Christian to love his enemy in this way is important. His study suffers, however, from a too-narrow understanding of "vengeance" as seen in biblical thought. If we follow G. Mendenhall's conclusions, as I do, the problem area changes considerably. I reject, of course, the assumption that Paul is saying that the "plight of the enemy will be made worse" through the love of the Christian.[14] I cannot conceive that Paul would have thought that by eating and drinking with enemies the result would be severe pain of any kind for the enemy. What Paul's argument seems to be is that the fate of the enemy can be left safely in the hands of God who will eventually obtain the allegiance of all enemies when all will recognize his sovereignty (1 Cor. 15:24–26). God's "vengeance" is precisely to exert sovereignty over all. Paul's interest in eating with Gentiles (Gal. 2:11–14) and his concern about the way in which meals unite people (1 Corinthians 11; Romans 14) makes it very hard to believe that he might have said here that by Christians feeding their enemies they could add to their woes! That interpretation still owes too much to Augustine of Hippo and does not pay enough attention to Oriental practices, the human reality of eating with people, and the power that such an act has in defusing hostilities.

Victory Over the Enemy

The triumphalist note struck here by Paul must surely provide a clue to the whole appeal. Strong verbal links, as well as links of content, bind this material to the "Q" materials. Paul, writing before either Matthew or Luke, mirrors the same teaching on what is done by the Christian when, in spite of his best efforts, peace has been disrupted. Paul joins himself to the Greek tradition which affirms at times that even when evil is done, the good person steadfastly refuses to do evil in return and thus allows good an opportunity to overcome evil. Most securely he is rooted in Judaism which also affirms that good can overcome evil. Indeed throughout the *Testaments of the Twelve Patriarchs* this theme is repeated on numerous occasions and becomes the major motivating force for the devout person (T. Benj. 4:3; 5:4; T. Issach. 7:7; T. Jos. 18:2–3).

For Paul this conviction is grounded firmly in the victory of Jesus over death. When all the forces of evil assailed the one truly good man, evil spent its force and good conquered. Secure in that victory, Paul urged the same strategy on the believers in Rome. Jesus had eaten with his enemies and by doing so overcame evil. Paul invites the Romans to participate in the victory of Christ.

A similar admonition appears in 1 Thess. 5:15 without any prediction that good will conquer over evil. In 1 Peter 3:9 an admonition appears:

> Do not return [repay] evil for evil or reviling for reviling; but on the contrary, bless, for to this you have been called, that you may obtain a blessing.

In 1 Peter the outcome is not predicted but the case is built on hope. He assumes that such action flows out of the nature of one's calling. The lengthy quotation from Psalm 34 (vv. 13–17) which follows in 1 Pet. 3:10–12 seems to indicate that "turning from wrong and doing good, seeking peace and pursuing it" results in "good days" and the assurance that God will hear the prayers of those who live an upright life.

It has, moreover, been observed that for 1 Peter "enemy-love *is* a condition for final salvation" and that it is a legitimate moral motivation to say: "Make sure you fulfill the condition of love in order to inherit salvation."[15] The reason that Peter can say this without contradicting Paul is that he orients his discussion of enemy-love around hope, whereas for Paul the center seems to have been faith. It would seem obvious, however, that both Paul and Peter are providing motivation for enemy-love. 1 Peter has been interpreted as stressing the gift of salvation as eschatological reality.[16] It would seem to me that it is also clearly seen as something which is *here* and is being realized among them. Thus while Paul stresses the victory of good over evil which takes place when the enemy is met with love: blessing, food, and so forth, 1 Peter joins loving the enemy with "seeking peace" in a degree of explicitness not found in any other biblical writer.

We misread 1 Peter if we project salvation into the distant future or into the next age. Salvation is here, and it takes the form of seeking peace by loving the enemy. We also misread him if we stress that the Christian is "inclined" not to seek his own honor, that he "cannot out of pride or anxiety return evil for evil or reviling for reviling" or that

Christians will merely be "inclined to bless those who revile them." Such language does a serious injustice to the force of 1 Peter's imperatives and the clear mandates of Jesus.[17]

It is evident that Paul is addressing the Romans on a critical point dealing with peace. It would be comforting to know that this has nothing to do with "national" enemies and that when it comes to such matters we need content ourselves only with quoting Rom. 13:1–6, words which have been used throughout the ages to encourage Christians to support their governments. We cannot ignore these clear words of Paul in Romans 12 or restrict them. They have the ring of authenticity and the echoes of the Master himself. Introducing, as they do, Paul's instruction on the need to respect authority, it is almost as if Paul first cites the commands of Jesus, always the Christians' supreme ruler. Immediately after the instruction on the state, he returns to the importance of love: "Leave no claim outstanding against you, except that of mutual love" (Rom. 13:8, NEB). Paul concludes this section on love with the admonition: "Let Christ Jesus himself be the armour that you wear; give no more thought to satisfying the bodily appetites" (13:14, NEB). Those translators who have retained the military metaphor (JB, NEB) have done so perhaps because of the word "armour" in v. 12. At any rate, they have caught the meaning of the admonition. In a society which boasted of the Pax Romana (the peace of Rome), which was maintained by force, Paul does not reject the military metaphor. He simply transforms it into the battle language of the Christian church.[18]

PEACE WITHIN THE COMMUNITY

Paul also deals with the central place which peace has within the fellowship at Rome. There are strong arguments for holding that Paul wrote Romans in order to bring peace between the Jewish and the Gentile Christians. At the least, we must take seriously Romans 14 and 15.[19] While Paul makes it clear that both the weak and the strong bear responsibility for the unity of the community, that conviction arises from a fundamental affirmation about the essence of the kingdom: "The kingdom of God is not eating and drinking, but justice, peace, and joy, inspired by the Holy Spirit" (Rom. 14:17, NEB). One can hardly be more basic than that. Paul's Jewishness affirms itself in all three of those values. Because he so strongly believes in them he urged the Romans to "pursue what makes for peace and for mutual upbuilding" (14:19). When all attributes are inspired by the Holy Spirit, oneness will result. In 2 Tim. 2:22 the writer urges Timothy to "turn from the wayward impulses of youth, and pursue justice, integrity, love, and peace with all who invoke the Lord in singleness of mind" (NEB). As in Romans, peace and justice stand side by side.

It is, however, not only the kingdom of God which consists of peace. God, too, is described as "the God of Peace" twice in the closing chapters of Romans (15:33; 16:20). In such a description Paul uses a favorite expression (1 Cor. 14:33; 2 Cor. 13:11; Phil. 4:9; 1 Thess. 5:23; 2 Thess. 3:16) which defines in a singular way for Paul what God's will is for the church and the world. The fact that the writer to the Hebrews also uses that expression (13:20) signifies that the phrase had popularity elsewhere in the church as well. It appears elsewhere apparently only in the *Testaments of the Twelve Patriarchs.*

Accordingly, one of the oldest songs of the Israelite people proclaiming that Yahweh is a warrior (Exodus 15) has been transformed. Like all of his Jewish contemporaries, Paul proclaimed that his God was the one who gives peace and desires it for all.

Peace Within the Family

There is clearly no desire on Paul's part to restrict peace in any way. It is not merely the inner peace of mind or soul with which our modern age is so enamored. Indeed the formula "peace of mind" is hardly to be found in the Bible. Peace takes shape in the most immediate of all human relations: the family.

It is in the context of the tensions that arise between believing and unbelieving spouses that Paul affirms: "God has called us to peace" (1 Cor. 7:15). Important as it is for the marital vows to be respected, Paul affirms here that *shalom,* wholeness of relationship, is more important. The ability to live together in harmony is a part of God's gift of peace. But, equally, Paul is saying that the Christian partner is under no compulsion and should allow the unbeliever the freedom to leave the union: God's call is a call to live in peace. This is a striking allowance for separation not found in Jesus but a normal outcome of Paul's view of the central gift of peace. Furthermore, Paul recognizes the changing conditions brought by the gospel when the wills of *both* parties are respected and the overarching call of God is kept in view.

At the same time he invites: "Think of it: as a wife you may be your husband's salvation; as a husband you may be your wife's salvation" (1 Cor. 7:16). Again Paul's strong hope affirms itself along similar lines to 1 Peter (3:1). When peacemakers live with others and have continuing daily contact with them, the possibility of wholeness is always there.

The same logic asserts itself in Paul's directives to the Corinthian church on what to do with the enthusiasts, the prophets and the women in 1 Corinthians. He bases his mandates on his conviction that God is not a god of confusion but of peace (1 Cor. 14:33).

Paul's view of peace, however, is christologically determined. The sentence, "for he [Christ] is our peace" (Eph. 2:14) and the admonition, "let the peace of Christ rule in your hearts, to which indeed you were called" (Col. 3:15), are Pauline even though they occur in letters rejected as Pauline by many scholars. Certainly few affirmations about this topic are as profound as the ones made in Ephesians 2. The Gentiles have exchanged their world without hope and without God for one in union with Christ Jesus. Distance, or being far off, has been exchanged for being brought near through the shedding of Christ's blood, "for he is our peace" (Eph. 2:14–18):

> Gentiles and Jews, he has made the two one, and in his own body of flesh and blood has broken down the enmity which stood like a dividing wall between them; for he has annulled the law with its regulations and rules so as to create out of the two a single new humanity in himself, thereby making peace. This was his purpose, to reconcile the two in a single body to God through the cross, on which he killed the enmity. So he came and proclaimed the good news: peace to you who were far off, and peace to those who were near by (au. trans.).

No other statement so strongly affirms the central place which peace holds in Paul's thinking, and none is so clearly based in the nature, person, and work of Christ. The peacemaking role attributed to the disciples in Matt. 5:9 is here grounded in Christ. It is the cross and not the resurrection which forms the basis of Paul's views on peace.[20]

The peace of Christ binds the Christian community together (Eph. 4:3): in short, the writer is saying "spare no effort to keep the oneness of the Spirit in the bond of peace." The Colossians are told: "Let the peace that Christ gives guide you in the decisions you make; for together in the one body God called you to this peace" (Col. 3:15, au. trans.).

This peace is not to be equated with human ingenuity or human efforts to remain calm. It transcends all human understanding. It surpasses both human emotions and human reason. It is in Christ Jesus, and he too lived contrary to human reason and a life superior to human wisdom. It may, therefore, more often than not also stand directly opposed to human schemes and plans to bring peace. Ultimately it is the cure to all human anxiety when "in everything we make our requests known to God in prayer and petition with thanksgiving. Then the peace of God, which is worth far more than human reasoning will protect our hearts and thoughts in Christ Jesus" (Phil. 4:6–7, au. trans.).

The Armor of Christ

In the Letter to the Ephesians the most extensive symbolic usage of military metaphors appears. Although it is not considered Pauline, it is worthy of some analysis. The Christian life is described in terms of a battle, a battle not against humans but against superhuman forces of evil (Eph. 6:12). The source of strength is in the Lord and in his mighty power (6:10). Twice he warns his readers to put on *God's* armor (6:10, 13) and he specifies it in detail. The uniqueness of that armor is at once apparent when we compare it with a similar text in the Book of the Wisdom of Solomon, a source certainly familiar to Paul.

Wisdom 5		*Ephesians 6*
Of Wrath	ARMOR	God's
All Creation	WEAPON	
Justice	CUIRASS	Justice
Doom inflexible	HELMET	Salvation
Holiness	SHIELD	Faith
Bolts of Lightning	BOW	
Relentless Anger	SWORD	Word of God

Resentment,   ARTILLERY
fury of hail

BOOTS   Peace, Gospel of

The contrasts in these two lists are striking. We must bear in mind that while the author of the book of Wisdom is describing the armor God wears, the author prescribes God's own armor for the Christians. In Wisdom God's armor is described as being one of zeal (Wisd. of Sol. 5:17), his relentless anger *(orgē)* will be sharpened as a sword (5:20); and the artillery of his resentment *(thymos)* shall let fly a fury of hail (5:22). None of these terms appears in the list in Ephesians. They are not seen as part of the Christian armor even though in another place in Ephesians the author instructs them "be angry, but do not sin" (4:26). The author could very well have been thinking about Isa. 59:17 which also speaks of God's intervention:

> He put on righteousness as a breastplate,
>   and a helmet of salvation upon his head;
> he put on garments of vengeance for clothing,
>   and wrapped himself in fury as a mantle.

If he was indeed thinking about this verse, the contrast could not be sharper. The theme of vengeance is missing totally here in Ephesians and the reference to being shod with peace (6:15) may allude to Isa. 52:7, although it is applied more concretely to the Christians to whom he is writing. They are, in effect, the messengers of peace expected by Isaiah.

Whereas the Wisdom of Solomon and Isaiah have a human foe in mind (the former: those who persecute the righteous; the latter: the people of Israel who do not intervene), Ephesians consistently views the battle as one that is not fought against a human foe. Thus, an important clue to human struggle against injustice is provided. Liberation movements marshall their forces to unseat rulers and to remove corrupt officials and those who gouge the poor. But killing or removing the oppressors does not necessarily remove oppression. More often if the means used are violent, it merely opens the door to other oppressors.

To acknowledge this reality does not make our efforts less intensive. We are simply able to identify the target more accurately. Above all, we are able to recognize the foes against whom we fight: bigotry, fear, selfishness, intolerance, violence, and cheapening of life are foes which reside in us as well. For the demonic powers can dwell in us as well as in the ones we consider our foes. No one has a monopoly on evil. If it is evil we wish to eradicate rather than what we consider to be evil people, then it is quite a different battle. That battle is always begun in ourselves.

For Ephesians the battle seems to be largely a defensive one. Four times the author urges: "Stand!" (6:11, 13, 14). For this the boots of peace are particularly important. This may be a fulfillment of those great words from Isaiah (9:5):

> For every boot of the tramping
>   warrior in battle tumult
> and every garment rolled in blood
> will be burned as fuel for the fire.

The feet shod with the good news of peace will provide a firm footing (Eph. 6:15). In that sense peace is what it is all about: not peace after we have doled out justice and vengeance; not peace after we have taken all the territory we want and nailed down our claim to it by secure borders. The peace, rather, which is clad in justice: wholeness of encounter which takes place when we speak the truth in love. The shoes of peace walk all over God's earth. They are not confined to any country which feels itself chosen by God. All people who find their rest in God and place their trust in God's way of peacemaking can enter into this struggle and hear the good news of this peace.

The sword is the one given by the Spirit: the words of God. Like Jesus, the follower has no other weapon than the word of God which heals all wounds. This weapon is not used for cutting people down but for building them up.

If the resource of strength is the Lord, the way in which that resource is made available is through prayer: "Give yourselves wholly to prayer and entreaty; pray on every occasion in the power of the Spirit" (Eph. 6:18, NEB).

We speak a good deal about praying for peace. The biblical writers don't put it quite that way. Every greeting, especially the one given the enemy, is for them a prayer for peace. Every blessing is also a prayer for peace. And at least one biblical writer stresses the fact that

Christians are to offer petitions, prayers, intercessions, and thanksgivings for *all;* for sovereigns and those in high office, that we may lead a quiet and peaceable life (1 Tim. 2:1–2). We do not pray only for our governments but for *all* who are in authority. Every protest against policies of governments should be undergirded and bathed with that kind of prayer.

Such an admonition to prayer assumes, however, an active and aggressive role in the peacemaking process. Prayer is never meant to be a last resort or a substitute for action but rather the one supreme action which undergirds and focuses all else. It is an affirmation that whatever is done must be motivated by God's love and is barren without God's attendant blessing. To believe in the power of prayer is to affirm that God is alive and deeply involved in the process of history.[21] To pray for rulers in another country is to acknowledge God's sovereignty over all and to recognize God's love for all. It is not to ignore injustices and differences of degrees of evil. It is merely to recognize that God alone is judge and that we must all answer to God. It is God's battle and we are under God's exclusive command.

NOTES

1. On the Pauline development of this theme Ulrich Luz, *Eschatologie und Friedenshandeln bei Paulus* (Stuttgart: Katholisches Bibelwerk, 1981), chapter by Luz, 153–93; E. Brandenburger, *Frieden im neuen Testament* (Gütersloh: Gerd Mohn, 1973), 51–67 [in a slightly different form in *Wort und Dienst: Jahrbuch der kirchlichen Hochschule Bethel*, N.F. 11, (1971): 58–72]. Erich Dinkler (*Eirēnē* [Heidelberg: Carl Winter, 1973], 23ff.) concludes: "If it was said in antiquity: *Eirēnē* is peace, she does not bring it—then it was said, if we summarize in an inescapable manner, among early Christians, Jesus Christ *is* peace—he has freely granted it and demands that the gift of peace as reconciling act of God in Christ be offered to the world" (p. 46). See also Peter Stuhlmacher, " 'Er ist unser Friede' (Eph. 2:14)," in *Neues Testament und Kirche,* ed. Joachim Gnilka (Freiburg: Herder, 1974): 337–58; Joseph Comblin, *Theologie des Friedens* (Vienna: Styria, 1963); Siegfried Meurer, *Das Recht im Dienst der Versöhnung und des Friedens* (Zürich: Theologischer Verlag, 1972); Victor Furnish, *The Love Command in the New Testament* (Nashville: Abingdon Press, 1972), 91–131; and Vernard Eller, *War and Peace From Genesis to Revelation* (Scottdale, Pa.: Herald Press, 1981).

2. For the critical aspects of this theme and a careful discussion, see Stuhlmacher, " 'Er ist unser Friede' (Eph. 2:14)," 338. See E. Käsemann, "A

Primitive Christian Baptismal Liturgy," in *Essays on New Testament Themes* (London: SCM Press, 1964; Philadelphia: Fortress Press, 1982), 152 n. 1. "The Christian belongs not to the cosmos, but to the Cosmocrator." The Christian "has cast off dependence on the forces which govern this world and is subject from now on solely to the Son, *whose empire is defined by the forgiveness of sins*" (162), my italics.

3. R. Bultmann, *Theology of the New Testament* (New York: Charles Scribner's Sons; London: SCM Press, 1952), 1:286–87. For Bultmann, " 'we have peace' (Rom. 5:1) only unfolds the meaning of righteousness."

4. Basic to our understanding of curse and blessing in the Bible is still, Lyder Brun, *Segen und Fluch im Urchristentum* (Oslo: Dybwad, 1932): "We cannot doubt that the blessing actually was seen as a weapon against the curse, that the blessing of God and of Christ which the Christians themselves have experienced has placed them in a position to bless their enemies and to greet them" (34). Now also Claus Westermann, *Blessing in the Bible and the Life of the Church*, ET: Keith R. Crim (Philadelphia: Fortress Press, 1978): "The Christianization here consists in the breaking of the old contrast between blessing and curse. This exhortation enables the Christian to lead an existence in which the blessing on our fellowman no longer has a limit formed by the cursing of our enemies" (99). See also, W. Schenk, *Der Segen im Neuen Testament* (Berlin: Evangelische Verlagsanstalt, 1967).

5. Here Paul is simply repeating what is the normative position in Judaism with respect to the dictum: "Do not repay evil with evil." See the copious documentation of this from such sources as *Pseudo-Phocylides* and the *Letter of Aristeas*. It is uniformly taught in the *Testament of The Twelve Patriarchs*. Others are provided in Andreas Nissen, *Gott und der Nächste im antiken Judentum*, 304–18. I disagree with his conclusion that it is not possible to speak of "love your enemies" in Judaism since actions described or prescribed are in many cases identical to what two other Jews, Jesus and Paul, prescribed when at least the former spoke of "loving the enemy" (see Nissen, *Gott und der Nächste*, 316). Likewise I consider it questionable that early Christians were the first to add a positive note to the admonition not to repay evil with evil.

6. See W. Klassen, " 'Humanitas' as seen by Epictetus and Musonius Rufus," *Studi Storico Religiosi* 1 (1977):63–82; also my essay, "A Child of Peace."

7. See Harold W. Attridge, *First-Century Cynicism in the Epistles of Heraclitus* (Chico, Calif.: Scholars Press, 1976), 30–33. The seventh epistle is a particularly strong appeal that war is something which animals avoid and that humans might well emulate animals in this area. Luise Schottroff ("Love of Enemies") has gathered much material from the popular philosophy of the Greco-Roman world on this topic.

8. A point made by the detailed study of the origins of Cynicism by Heinrich Niehues-Pröbsting, *Der Kynismus des Diogenes und der Begriff des*

Zynismus (Munich: W. Fink, 1979). One example of the Cynic shamelessness united to a concept of making oneself totally vulnerable to one's foe is found in Teles' discussion of self-sufficiency. He reports that Diogenes when being shoved and twisted did not put his neck under the yoke "but instead showed the fellow his penis, and says 'My dear sir, stand here in front of me and shove this.' " What Teles apparently wishes to show is that Diogenes dealt with harassment by making himself even more vulnerable. Is this a parallel to what Jesus instructs his disciples to do? See E. O'Neil, *Teles: The Cynic Teacher* (Chico, Calif.: Scholars Press, 1977), 11.

9. Ernst Käsemann, *Commentary on Romans* (Grand Rapids: Wm. B. Eerdmans, 1980), 348. His words, "Christians cannot themselves escape this shattering," came painfully true when his own daughter laid down her life in South America.

10. "The law of Hellenistic history and 'modern' man is retaliation." G. Gloege, *The Day of His Coming* (London: SCM Press, 1963), 195. With respect to the radical change which comes in this area in the biblical tradition, see George Mendenhall, *The Tenth Generation*, 69–104. See above, n. 7.

11. See my essay, "Coals of Fire: Sign of Repentance or Revenge?" *NTS* 9 (1963):337–50; see above, p. 36, where I have adopted the translation, "bring him to change."

12. As argued by Krister Stendahl, "Hate, Non-Retaliation and Love. 1QS x, 17–20 and Romans 12:19–21," *HTR* 55 (1962): 352. The discussion has to center on the meaning of "vengeance."

13. See Ladislaus J. Bolchazy, *Hospitality in Early Rome, Livy's Concept of its Humanizing Force* (Chicago: Ares, 1977). Livy praises Camillus for "He had conquered his enemies with justice and fair dealing" (71). See also 23, 63ff. for the law of hospitality versus war.

14. John Piper, *Love Your Enemies*, 111–19. Piper has great difficulty reconciling Paul's generous use of Old Testament texts to support enemy love because he has earlier (p. 91) described Jesus' love command as seen by a perceptive Jew as an "attack upon Torah." The problem comes out of an inadequate methodology, in particular a desire to make the love your enemies teaching a Christian creation rather than seeing it as part of Judaism.

15. John Piper, "Hope as the Motivation of Love: 1 Peter 3:9–12" *NTS* 26 (1980): 212–31, see 230.

16. Ibid., 212.

17. Piper (ibid., 217) indicates that he phrased those sentences carefully "so as not to imply that a Christian in absolutely every situation is forbidden to retaliate against evil" (fn. 24). By referring to 2:14 he suggests that the Christian is relieved of this mandate when it conflicts with being submissive to the authorities, so "the possible situation of forcefully resisting evil in the world cannot be ruled out even for the Christian. But even when he resists, it will be from a different spirit. . . ." By quoting Goppelt, who in turn relies on Luther, the straight command of Christ is accommodated to our present

thinking. Using this logic we could certainly assist any President to retaliate against the enemy after he has been defined as evil. It is particularly ironical that Piper who has so diligently traced this teaching back to Jesus himself, can after doing so, conclude that the "spirit" in which you do it is more important than whether you resist evil with force or with love; a conclusion not found in Jesus! Peter himself appeals not to the "spirit" but rather to the pattern traced by Jesus which we are to follow (1 Pet. 2:21). What John Yoder wrote of Carl F. H. Henry applies here: "he represents faithfully a tradition that has been able to appropriate much of the New Testament idiom without catching its central historical thrust" (*The Politics of Jesus* [Grand Rapids: Wm. B. Eerdmans, 1972], 131).

18. The old slogan, "If you want peace, prepare for war" was current already in his time. See Wolfgang Haase, " 'Si vis pacem, para bellum,' Zur Beurteilung militärischer Staerke in der römischen Kaiserzeit," *Akten des XI. Internationalen Limeskongresses* (Budapest: Hungarian Academy of Sciences, 1977), 721–55. For an excellent study of the way in which the early church dealt with this problem, see Adolf von Harnack, *Militia Christi*, ET: David McInnes Gracie (Philadelphia: Fortress Press, 1981) and Jean-Michel Hornus, *It Is Not Lawful for me to Fight* (Scottdale, Pa.: Herald Press, 1980). There has been agreement for some time that early Christians did not participate in the military. The argument revolves mainly around the question whether they refused by reason of commitment to nonviolence, or by reason of emperor worship. Gracie's introduction to the Harnack volume deals with all the critical issues.

19. Paul S. Minear, *The Obedience of Faith: The Purposes of Paul in the Epistle to the Romans* (London: SCM Press, 1971).

20. Alfred Juncker, (*Die Ethik des Apostel Paulus* [Halle: Niemeyer, 1919], 234) states: "Through the sacrificial death of Jesus and the strong emphasis Paul placed on it the love your enemies command has achieved such a central place in Christian devotion 'that you overthrow Christianity entirely if you reject love for the enemy' (Wendland)."

21. The call of the American bishops that there always be a petition for peace in the general intercessions at every Eucharistic celebration is to be welcomed.

Conclusion:
To Walk the
Paths of Peace

In January, 1982, a magazine had a special article on the effect of war on children. The writer concluded that children have a fierce will to survive "that sometimes takes the form of revenge, and at other times, of an abiding serenity."[1] What was remarkable about these portraits was the number of children who chose to reject revenge—or at least to think of it in wholly nonviolent terms. Thus a young lad from Cambodia vowed revenge, but not in the form that he would seek to track down the murderers of his loved ones. Rather, he would "take his revenge" by dedicating his life to nobler things.

We have seen that already ancient thought, including the Bible, began to take that position. Scholars have observed that there is a movement in the biblical themes from the rejection of revenge to love for enemies which leads to peace. The only lasting peace is one which goes through reconciliation. Even in apocalyptic literature (e.g., the *Assumption of Moses*) including the Book of Revelation, victory is achieved through the power of love not the love for power. The Lamb, central to the drama of that book, and either the direct or indirect figure who presides over all that happens, is for that community the clue to the meaning of history. The Lamb is a figure central to the early church in its struggle with the enemy. Early Christians were convinced that they would conquer together with the Lamb and share in his victory. Although vengeance is a central theme in the Book of Revelation, we need to look carefully at the biblical meaning of vengeance in terms of establishment of the divine rule or *imperium*. Then we cannot dismiss the book as filled with hatred and as denying all that is said in the rest of the Bible about love your enemies. The

Lamb's vengeance is to take all hatred and murder unto himself. He is worthy because he was slain (Rev. 5:12).[2]

If biblical scholars have become more involved in these issues, far more so have the churches: for example, the Roman Catholic Bishops of the United States culminating in their statement (*The Challenge of Peace*, 1983) and the World Council of Churches meeting at Vancouver, 1983. There is, moreover, an amazing awakening among those churches which have traditionally been considered in the 'evangelical' camp but have often been, and still are to a large extent, aligned with militant postures, directed especially against what is seen as such "godless" foes as China or the Soviet Union.[3]

Let it be said very clearly and explicitly: to be for peace or to love one's enemies does not signify that one supports the political systems of the countries designated as enemies. To work in the peace movement—or for that matter to be a member of the church—is to be aligned with the Prince of Peace, and choices between political systems are secondary to that allegiance. As followers of Jesus, peace children are slow to condemn. Even when major international incidents take place it generally takes weeks or months to discover who was responsible. It is far more complicated than to try to allocate responsibility in a confrontation among children on a playground or colleagues working in an office.

Furthermore, it needs to be stressed that there is now an amazing confluence of humanity's self-interest and the deepest moral teachings of Judaism and Christianity. Perhaps it has always been the case that *agape* had the strongest potential for self-fulfillment and survival while being directed towards the needs of the neighbor and the enemy. As our world shrinks we become aware that the destiny of each becomes the destiny of all. Far from bringing us to the brink of war, those who call for disarmament and a de-escalation of the arms race may be the only voices which speak sanely now a word which, if heeded, can save the human race. Such convictions come not from pride but rather from the grim realities which we face today. They also are grounded in the faith that God does not want to destroy the world but to save it. Above all, for religious people it is important that the values which stand at the center of biblical religion be allowed to express themselves in our actions in this very important sphere of life.

Many Christians have been misled by the predictions of the Bible that there will always be war. As wars multiply this is cited as evidence that the end is near. Since war is an eternal reality, part of the divine intention and plan, why work to end war?

When Admiral Douglas Boyle retired from the Canadian Navy, he expressed what many people feel about war: "I have always said that in the military our job is to kill. And we must do it better than anyone else. Besides the Bible says there will be wars and rumors of wars" (CBC Interview 7/10/77). Just because biblical writers (Mark 14:7; Matt. 26:11; John 12:8) indicate that there will always be poor among us does not mean that we do nothing to alleviate poverty. Just because the writer of 2 Timothy describes eighteen conditions which will abound during the time of troubles, which he calls the "the last days," does not mean that we do not seek to avoid those conditions (2 Tim. 3:1–5).

It is important to note that each reference to war in the time of the end warns the hearers *not* to conclude that the end is upon them (Matt. 24:6; Mark 13:7; Luke 21:9). The Day of the Lord comes like a thief in the night—"When the people say, 'There is peace and security,' then sudden destruction will come upon them as travail comes upon a woman with child, and there will be no escape" (1 Thess. 5:3). All witnesses agree that there are no clear clues to the time of the end and also agree in calling for watchfulness and faithfulness to the Lord during the interim. In the meantime we have the Lord's command: Love your enemies. Those who answer, "But it doesn't work" must be helped to see that every time it has truly been tried it has worked! It has reconciled foes; it has shown that good can overcome evil.

Firm in the conviction that Yahweh is Lord, and committed to the kingship of Jesus, the community whom he has called strives for peace. Every renunciation of violence and methods of coercion is accompanied by an invitation to a better way and a modeling of that way both within the Christian community and towards those outside.

It follows that all Christians must oppose with all the means at their disposal (and they are considerable) the readiness to use weapons—certainly nuclear weapons—against any other human being. For the readiness to do so is blasphemy, a presumption, "an indignity of monstrous proportions offered to God."[4] The precise form in which we work for peace will vary with each person. It must be suited to the gifts which God has given to each. Some will write and lobby and march and pray at places where our arsenals are located. Others will write letters to persons in authority; still others will raise their voices and votes in Parliaments and the Congress. Clergy will find again those great texts in the Bible which call us to pursue peace. Mothers will find ways of telling their children stories of great peacemakers and will assist their children in finding ways to resolve conflicts on the playground or in the home. Spouses will mirror the *shalom* of God in their relations to each other. All will, however, join in the awareness that we are called to be peace children—people whose origins are to be found in the nonviolent confrontation with evil expressed in God's love for the world when he gave his son in active love for his enemies. We are children of peace not only by virtue of origin but also by virtue of the goals for which we work.

With such a recovery of our identity, we march as warriors of peace facing the evils of this world squarely, but confident that the battle has already been won by the Lamb that was slain (Rev. 5:12). We can share in his victory only if we are prepared to suffer with him and to walk steadfastly on the way which he has laid out for us. This demands a strength of ego and, above all, a symbiosis with the Christ so that we can say with Paul (Gal. 2:20):

> I have been crucified with Christ; it is no longer I who live, but Christ who lives in me; and the life I now live in the flesh I live by faith in the Son of God, who loved me and gave himself for me. (Gal. 2:20).

Far from denying ego strength and far from leaving to evil the initiative in this way, the children of peace demonstrate their strength and their identity by keeping the initiative and setting the rules of the battle. Fused into one body of Christ we can then express God's love for all who live in this world.

Hope is in short supply these days within and outside the church. Is that because we have placed our hopes too often in political leaders who lead us blindly toward a confrontation with death even as they promise us peace and security? One writer several decades before Jesus, drawing both on Greek wisdom and Jewish theology, already saw that the best defense against the enemy is generosity. Let that be the treasure in your strong-room, Sirach urges (29:12–13), for "it will rescue you from all affliction; more than a mighty shield and more than a heavy spear."

The concept of loving the enemy and its relationship to peace has been shown to be a realistic solution to today's problems. There is a better way. We know what the build-up of weapons has led to in the past. We know what happens when we build on suspicion and hate and refuse to negotiate with those who are in opposite camps or whom we designate as enemies. What we do not know, but what we can surely begin to affirm now, is what will happen if we give the peace of Christ a chance. Surely, given the alternatives, it is worth a try. For the way of Christ calls to the deepest resources within the human spirit and represents the highest in both divine example and human dignity. It affirms the value of human life and forms a commitment to human existence missing in the further build-up of arms and the present course of diplomacy. Above all, it is in harmony with the Word of God which has spoken throughout Jewish and Christian history. The way of peace represents, therefore, the good news for our day as it has in many days past, and if heeded, will for many days to come.

NOTES

1. *Time* 1/11/82; 24. See the longer treatment with extensive quotes, Roger Rosenblatt, *Children of War* (New York: Doubleday, 1983).

2. See "Vengeance in the Apocalypse of John," *CBQ* 28 (1966): 300–316 and Adela Yarbro Collins, "The Political Perspective of the Revelation to John," *JBL* 96 (1977): 241–56. I consider it one of the unfortunate ironies of our century that two figures who have done much to enrich our appreciation of the meaning of symbols and have given considerable thought to the meaning of the book have so fundamentally misrepresented it: See C. G. Jung, *Answer to Job,* ET: R. F. C. Hull (Cleveland: World Pub., 1961) and D. H. Lawrence, *Apocalypse* (Middlesex: Penguin, 1974; first published, 1931).

3. *Sojourners* magazine represents a vital force today in bringing evangelicals into this discussion. See, among others, Jim Wallis, *Waging Peace: A Handbook for Abolishing Nuclear Weapons* (New York: Harper & Row, 1982); Ronald Sider, *Christ and Violence* (Scottdale, Pa.: Herald Press, 1979); Vernard Eller, *War and Peace, From Genesis to Revelation* (Scottdale, Pa.: Herald Press, 1981); Don Kraybill, *Facing Nuclear War: A Plea for Christian Witness* (Scottdale, Pa.: Herald Press, 1982). In many ways still the

most seminal work is John Howard Yoder's *The Politics of Jesus* (Grand Rapids: Wm. B. Eerdmans, 1972). It is simply impossible for evangelicals or any student of the Bible to overlook the political dimensions of Jesus' teaching and life after Yoder. Yoder, as a committed Mennonite active in World Council circles and teaching in a Catholic university (Notre Dame), has been able to catch the ear of the evangelicals in a singular way. When Yoder, a systematic theologian who trained under Barth, asserts that evangelicals "represent faithfully the tradition that has been able to appropriate much of the New Testament idiom without catching its central historical thrust" (131), he has placed his finger on a fundamental weakness. Disclaiming all originality and competence in biblical studies (224), Yoder has nevertheless set the agenda for the discussion.

4. George Kennan, *The Nuclear Delusion* (New York: Pantheon Books, 1982), 206–7.

Suggestions
for Further Reading

Alley, Rewi. *Peace Through the Ages: Translations from the Poets of China*. Peking, 1954. Selected stories indicating that revenge can be overcome and when it is, peace is restored.

Baldry, H. C. *The Unity of Mankind in Greek Thought*. Cambridge: Cambridge Univ. Press, 1965. An expert treatment of developments which allowed Greek thought to treat women, slaves, and barbarians as part of a unified mankind.

Bigelow, Robert. *The Dawn Warriors: Man's Evolution Toward Peace*. Boston: Little Brown & Co., 1969. By demonstrating that war was coterminous with humankind he also points out that people can learn to cooperate to bring about peace.

Brandon, S. G. F. *Jesus and the Zealots*. Manchester: Manchester Univ. Press, 1967. The standard work which argues that early Christians as a reaction to the fall of Jerusalem, made Jesus who had zealot tendencies into a pacific Christ.

Brown, Robert McAfee. *Making Peace in the Global Village*. Philadelphia: Westminster Press, 1981. A superb introduction to the major issues, designed for group study.

Daube, David. *Civil Disobedience in Antiquity*. Edinburgh: Edinburgh Univ. Press, 1972. An important study citing numerous cases of nonviolent protest in antiquity.

Eller, Vernard. *War and Peace—From Genesis to Revelation*. Scottdale, Pa.: Herald Press, 1980. An extremely well written summary of the theme in biblical literature.

Erikson, E. *Gandhi's Truth*. New York: W. W. Norton, 1969. The best application of the psycho-analytical method to a great peacemaker of the twentieth century.

Erlander, Daniel. *By Faith Alone: A Lutheran Looks at the Bomb*. Chelan, Wash.: Holden Village, 1982. A popular study from a Lutheran perspective.

Ferguson, John. *War and Peace in the World's Religions*. New York: Oxford

Univ. Press, 1978. A timely selection of and commentary on texts bearing on this issue from many religions.

Freyne, Sean. *Galilee From Alexander the Great to Hadrian.* Wilmington, Del.: Michael Glazier, 1980. Basic to our understanding of the background of Jesus.

Gouldner, A. W. *The Hellenic World.* Boston: Beacon Press, 1969. Important study of the contest model in ancient society.

Gray, J. Glenn. *The Warriors: Reflections on Men in Battle.* New York: Harper & Row, 1959. Classic statement of meaning of "enemy" from a war veteran and sociologist.

Hammer, P. L. *Shalom in the New Testament.* Philadelphia: United Church Press, 1973.

———. *The Gift of Shalom: Bible Studies in Human Life and the Church.* Philadelphia: United Church Press, 1976. Both of the Hammer books are based on careful research. Written for congregational study.

Harnack, Adolf von. *Militia Christi: The Christian Religion and the Military in the First Three Centuries.* ET, David McInnes Gracie. Philadelphia: Fortress Press, 1981. Basic work in the field by an acknowledged master.

Hastings, James, ed. *The Christian Doctrine of Peace.* Edinburgh: T. & T. Clark, 1922. A thorough and judicious attempt by a scholar of first rank to develop a theology of peace during the first World War.

Hengel, Martin. *Victory Over Violence: Jesus and the Revolutionists.* Introduction by Robin Scroggs. Philadelphia: Fortress Press, 1973. An authority on the Zealots applies his knowledge to the issue of peace.

———. *Was Jesus a Revolutionist?* Facet Books. Philadelphia: Fortress Press, 1971. An answer to Brandon and others who argue Jesus' zealot connections.

Hirsch, R. G. *Thy Most Precious Gift: Judaism in Pursuit of Peace.* New York: Union of Hebrew Congregations, 1974. Best brief description of peace in Judaism.

Hornus, Jean-Michel. *It Is Not Lawful for me to Fight: Early Christian Attitudes toward War, Violence, and the State.* Scottdale, Pa.: Herald Press, 1980. The most important book on the early church and war. (French ed., 1960).

Kennan, George. *The Nuclear Delusion.* New York: Pantheon Books, 1982. One of the foremost world statesmen, who knows Russia, argues for sanity in our approach.

MacQuarrie, John. *The Concept of Peace.* New York: Harper & Row, 1973. Peace is treated from a philosophical perspective.

Minear, Paul. *Commands of Christ.* Nashville: Abingdon Press, 1972. A provocative and refreshing way of looking at Jesus' teaching.

Piper, John. *Love Your Enemies: Jesus' Love Command in the Synoptic Gospels and the Early Christian Paranesis.* SNTSMS 38. Cambridge: Cambridge Univ. Press, 1979. An excellent study of this commandment.

Marred by a failure to appreciate Jewish and Greek background and by a naive view of authority.

Sider, Ronald J. *Christ and Violence*. Scottdale, Pa.: Herald Press, 1979. Good discussion of this issue for congregations of conservative bent.

Swartley, Willard. *Slavery, Sabbath, War and Women*. Scottdale, Pa.: Herald Press, 1983. See esp. Chap. 3, pp. 96–149. Presents a masterful summary of the pacifist as well as the nonpacifist position.

Swain, J. Carter. *War, Peace and the Bible*. Maryknoll, N.Y.: Orbis Books, 1982. A good discussion of the issues meant for lay persons.

Wallis, Jim, ed. *Waging Peace: A Handbook for the Struggle to Abolish Nuclear Weapons*. New York: Harper & Row, 1982. A very valuable tool for those interested in reflection and action.

Weigel, Richard D. and Matthew Melko. *Peace in the Ancient World*. Jefferson, N.C.: MacFarland, 1981. Demonstrates that peace was observed by large geographical areas over long periods of time in the ancient world.

Yoder, John Howard. *The Politics of Jesus*. Grand Rapids: Wm. B. Eerdmans, 1972. A most seminal work in looking at Jesus as a historical figure and peace maker.

Zampaglione, G. *The Idea of Peace in Antiquity*. ET, Richard Dunn. Notre Dame, Ind.: Univ. of Notre Dame Press, 1973. A valuable noncritical collection of sources but not precise in definitions nor fully representative.

Index

OLD TESTAMENT

OTHER WORKS